Golden Message

A Guide to Spiritual Life
With Self-Study Program
For Learning the Integral Way

Adapted by Maoshing Ni and Daoshing Ni
from the teachings of their father,
NI, HUA-CHING
Teachers of Natural Spiritual Truth

The Shrine of the Eternal Breath of Tao
College of Tao and Traditional Chinese Healing
SANTA MONICA

Thanks and appreciation to Suta Cahill,
Janet DeCourtney, Frank Gibson and the students
in the Atlanta Center, Karina Herring and
Blair Taylor for their assistance in typing, editing,
proof-reading and typesetting this book.

Shrine of the Eternal Breath of Tao
College of Tao and Traditional Chinese Healing, 1314 Second St. #208,
Santa Monica, CA 90401

Library of Congress Cataloging-In-Publication Data

Ni, Maoshing.
    Golden message : with self-study program for learning the
integral way / adapted by Maoshing Ni and Daoshing Ni
from the teachings of their father, Ni, Hua-Ching.
        p.   cm.
    Includes index.
    ISBN 0-937064-36-X : $11.95
    1. Spiritual formation. 2. Taoism.   I. Ni, Daoshing. II.
Ni, Hua Ching. III. Title.
BL1923.N536   1992   90-61067
299'.514448--dc20   CIP

Dedicated to those who wish to embrace
the Universal Soul - the Subtle Essence -
and align their thoughts and life
in the center of this unity.

To female readers,

According to natural spiritual teaching, male and female are equally important in the natural sphere. This is seen in the diagram of Tai Chi. Thus, discrimination is not practiced in our tradition. All my work is dedicated to both genders of human people.

Wherever possible, constructions using masculine pronouns to represent both sexes are avoided; where they occur, we ask your tolerance and spiritual understanding. We hope that you will take the essence of my teaching and overlook the superficiality of language. Gender discrimination is inherent in English; ancient Chinese pronouns do not have differences of gender. I wish that all of you achieve above the level of language or gender.

Thank you, H. C. Ni

Warning - Disclaimer

This book presents information and techniques that have been in use throughout the orient for many years. These practices utilize a natural system within the body; however, there are no claims for effectiveness. The information offered is to the author's best knowledge and experience and is to be used by the reader(s) at their own discretion and liability. It can be beneficial or harmful depending upon one's stage of development.

Because of the sophisticated nature of the information contained within this book, it is recommended that the reader also study the author's other books for further understanding of a healthy lifestyle and energy-conducting exercises. You need to accept legal responsibility for doing a thing you do not thoroughly understand.

Because people's lives have different conditions and different stages of growth, no rigid or strict practice can be applied universally. Thus, it must be through the discernment of the reader that the practices are selected. The adoption and application of the material offered in this book is totally your own responsibility.

The author and publisher of this book are not responsible in any manner for any injury that may occur through following the instructions in this book.

Contents

Prelude

The Subtle Essence conveyed by the teaching of the Integral Way is the deep truth of all religions, yet it leaves all religions behind to be the clothing of different seasons or worn in different places. The teaching of the Subtle Essence includes all things of religious importance, yet it is not on the same level as religion. It serves people's lives directly as all religions wish to do, but it surpasses the boundary of all religions and extracts the essence of all religions.

The Subtle Essence as conveyed by the teaching of the Integral Way is also the goal of all serious science, but it leaves all sciences behind as partial and temporal descriptions of this Integral Truth. Unlike any of the partial sciences, it goes beyond the level of any single scientific search.

The Subtle Essence is the master teaching. However, it does not rely on any authority. It is like a master key which can unlock all doors leading to the inner room of the ultimate truth directly. It is not frozen at the emotional surface of life and does not remain locked at the level of thought or belief with the struggling which extends to skepticism and endless searching.

The teaching of the Subtle Essence presents the core of the Integral Truth and helps you reach it yourself.

The Teaching of the Integral Way

Master Ni's teaching:

T   *stands for Truth*

A   *stands for Above*

O   *stands for Oneself*

Thus, Tao stands for TRUTH ABOVE ONESELF.

Also,

T   *stands for Truth*

A   *stands for Among*

O   *stands for Ourselves*

Thus, at the same time, Tao stands for
TRUTH AMONG OURSELVES.

Part 1

The Integral Way

I

In his books, our father Master Ni has often stated that the Integral Way is not Taoism but is the cream gathered from millions of years of human life experience and activity. It developed from the vast background of all kinds of spiritual activities commonly called Taoism, which is close to shamanism. Religious Taoism could be considered a folk religion. Thus, religious Taoism, like any other religion, is a matter of custom formed during many generations.

The Integral Way is not based on regional custom. It is spiritual development and achievement. It searches for the truth behind all human activities and concentrates particularly on the study and practice of a good human life rather than on the lives of plants and animals. The Integral Way is a proven method which can help one reach important human achievements. It teaches how to live a correct, balanced life without absolute allegiance to any local customs or religious activities. By following the Integral Way, you can independently accomplish a good, healthy life.

The Integral Way is what our grandparents promoted and our father continued. We too will continue these valuable teachings and practices that our predecessors gathered and distilled to support our growth.

The Integral Way goes beyond the narrow sense of tradition, sect or lineage to make life the central focus of all good achievement: your own life and other people's lives. This knowledge is both helpful and necessary for broadening and deepening your vision, your understanding and your reach. It is different from general Taoism, which has its temples, priests and deities but which lacks recognition of internal knowledge, as do all religions.

Our father's teaching can easily be confused with religious Taoism because people in the West do not know what Taoism is. After they have read our something by Master Ni, most people think Taoism is the same as our father's teachings. Although his pure spiritual teaching does not break away from the Western concept of religion, it serves as a profound spiritual education rather than a narrow religion with formalized doctrines. It is the intention of the Integral Way to support the growth of all people.

While integration means to be complete without leaving anything out, it also means eliminating things that affect your unity, such as conceptual activities or involvement in the emotional and trivial aspects of practical life.

When our father teaches, he always likes to use the words "teaching of Tao" or "learning of Tao" to distinguish his approach from the general concept of Taoism. To avoid this confusion, he uses the term "The Integral Way." As sons and students who are continuing his work, we too think it is important to clarify the Integral Way that was taught by our predecessors: it contains only the essence of all developed teachings rather than the external formalities of organization and structure.

In this chapter, we would like to quote what our father, Ni, Hua-Ching, has told us on different occasions to clarify the difference between the Integral Way and Taoism.

The Integral Way Follows The Secret of Human Spirits

Religious promotion, mythology, imagination and structure have all caused confusion about spirits. Few people actually know the secret of human spirits, which are human energy.

Basically, if you apply your own human energy to the pursuit of power, whether political or social, you may have such power. If you apply it to material expansion, then you may have all types of property or possessions. If you apply this energy to intellectual pursuits, then you may possess a certain amount of knowledge. Nevertheless, with regard to power, property and knowledge, most people are confused as to what is right and wrong, useful and useless, meaningful and meaningless.

Human spirits are the natural foundation of life. However, through generations, people's cultural life slowly deviated from that foundation. The ancient spiritually achieved ones were definitely different than people who developed religion. The common foundation of religion is the establishment of something external as a spiritual object in which to believe, worship and depend upon. All such objects are creations of the mind. The ancient spiritually achieved ones experienced confusion from worldly cultural creations such as religions, and they knew that all those creations were deviations from the truth rather than the original truth itself. Instead of pursuing religious customs, ancient spiritually achieved ones pursued original life spirits, which are the spirits of nature.

In the above paragraphs, the word "spirits" can be replaced by the word "God" by those of you who are so inclined. Please do not interpret the word "God" in the context of following God, serving God or dying for God. Those activities are not related to the reality of life spirits. All people have life spirits, but not all people conceive of an external God as a ruler. That concept is a great deviation from the truthful unity of all life. The recognition and the recognized are one in the deepest spiritual reality.

As a teacher or student of the natural spiritual truth, our father never considered himself a follower of Taoist religion and does not encourage people to follow the direction of the Taoist religion. After experiencing the divergence and deviation of various religious expressions, he yearns for and pursues the originality of human spirits, or the originality of the life spirits of all people.

People's lives are spiritual extensions of nature. The education of the Integral Way which our father, Ni, Hua-Ching, cherishes is different from mere faith in God or religious ritual. It requires seeing the healthy, upright spirit of life in each engagement and undertaking of life.

We have mentioned that each person has spiritual energy which can be guided and applied in one direction or another. The most essential point is the pure spiritual energy of a person's life before he or she extends or projects it in one direction or another or into one thing or another.

We cherish the originality of life spirit and hope that our friends with the same understanding will work on supporting each other's self-development, spiritual growth and individual spiritual cultivation, whether doing spiritual self-cultivation or group study.

Each individual who is born into the world is spiritually self-sufficient. People do not realize that it is not necessary to rely on anything or anyone during the long learning process of life, nor do they realize that it is not necessary to rely upon any idea or image. Spiritually, each person has everything needed to make the journey of life. Although we are dependent upon other people to varying degrees and in varying ways during all moments of our lives, we do not need to be dependent upon religious images and ideas to meet our spiritual needs. Through personal effort and refinement, a person can build spiritual sufficiency and enjoy personal spiritual attainment.

Spiritual achievement does not mean attaining something outside oneself. It means using the external environment with openness to gain awakening and enlightenment. After many years of cultivation, a person may discover that spiritual sufficiency has been achieved. Nothing external has become the master of one's life. Such an individual has attained spiritual self-mastery.

With this understanding, an individual would extend oneself to others. One would offer help in general contact with people rather than through the formality of religions. Other people are protected from being tricked by such a self-recovered healthy individual because he needs no god or policeman to keep watch over his behavior.

Spiritual truth is not external. Religious education may produce an external effect which affects the internal, but that is not truthful. Spiritual reality, in truth, is internal. Spiritual reality can be externalized as religion, and when this is not over done, it can be a healthy, good religion. Yet, what religion is not over done!

When internal spiritual reality is applied to worldly pursuits, it brings money, social influence or power through good and honest means. Spiritual reality can be externalized as the correct expression of the power of righteousness, propriety or suitability.

The spiritual energy of an individual can be externalized as knowledge. This knowledge is typically serviceable and helpful.

In all, everything is a manifestation of individual spiritual energy. Just like a flower or fruit which represents a plant, all behavior is the spiritual expression of an individual. By segmenting worship and ritual from the daily lives of people, religions have not truthfully served human spiritual growth, because such growth does not take place only one hour a week when a person is in church. Religions establish ideology, and ideology blocks or cuts off the connection between oneself and one's own individual spiritual nature and way of life.

If there is one important truth that our father has revealed to us, it is to reach the originality of your life spirits and to maintain the originality of healthy life spirits in handling all aspects and all behavior in life. This is the Integral Way. If you think that the Integral Way is something other than this, you are being fooled by religious propaganda.

Religion states that Tao offers protection and prosperity in life. This statement is true, but it means that these things come from yourself rather than an external "Tao."

Our father taught in China and in the West through lectures and writing. One of the main tenets of his teaching is that the Integral Way does not take advantage of people like religious work does. Religious Taoism was established and developed less than 2,000 years ago in China. However, the Integral Way continues the original search of ancient people for pure spiritual growth and development. The Integral Way is not a cultural construct that makes people paint their faces to such an extent that no one knows who they are any more. The simplicity of spiritual reality is not like painted cultural creations which confuse people.

II

A few truly talented individuals are born in each generation, and the human condition expresses itself both positively and negatively through the influence or aggravation of these talented individuals. Throughout many generations there are different kinds of talent. In order to extend a positive influence, a positive, talented person must learn to be firm and strong, not easily bent by external influences.

Talented young people need to find a good direction in which to work devotedly and whole-heartedly. Just as a small pond cannot raise a powerful dragon, living in a limited place causes limited growth. Yet, opportunity is everywhere, and it is possible to develop oneself anywhere.

In worldly life, learning to take pressure is almost a lifetime lesson or job in itself. Spiritual learning is not an escape from the pressures of life, although some conventional books would lead you to think so. Living an upright, firm life requires spiritual cultivation. Emotionally dependent people become religious followers, not spiritual achievers.

III

The Integral Way, the natural spiritual truth, is the subtle essence of universal life in all lives and all things. Learning the natural spiritual truth is a matter of spiritual development. It takes development to recognize the existence of the subtle essence and to embrace that subtle essence more than anything else. Thus, a school of thought and practices has been formed around the ability to develop oneself to know the subtle essence. Our father, Ni, Hua-Ching, is a student and a teacher of such a school.

Although we refer to the word "thought," the teaching of the Integral Way is actually non-conceptional and unrelated to thought. Thought or thinking is considered the formation and action of one level of subtle energy. However, the practice of the Integral Way values no thought or verbal description. It values the direct experience of reality which needs no interpretative activity of the mind. The mind tends to separate the original unity into parts. Reality does not need the mind to interpret or segment it into concepts. Nevertheless, it takes a lot of written work or explanation to convey what the subtle truth actually is. Yet, one person may describe the subtle truth to another, who may understand the words without actually having experienced the subtle truth. Words and symbols are not the purpose of this teaching, which presents the useful practices of each generation that can assist the health of mind, body and spirit and thereby restore our original unity.

The majority of Chinese people have followed a religion called Taoism for more than 2,000 years. It is more popular in some times and some places than in others. Taoist priests and Masters do not necessarily teach the Integral Way, although both share the word "Tao." Although our father, Ni, Hua-Ching, has been called a "Taoist Master" in the past, he is not a master or teacher in the same genre as religious Taoism. Master Ni only serves as a teacher of natural spiritual truth or whatever name fits the original teaching of the Integral Way and our own truthful practices.

Our father is also not the type of Taoist priest who wears red robes with golden embroidery, sitting or standing on a tall platform among worshippers and performing rituals. Our father continues the tradition of those who live an honest everyday life, yet who have a life spirit which is not limited to any one time or region. They embrace the universe and set no boundary for spiritual achievement. The constancy of nature is the foundation of their lives. We refer to them as spiritually developed ones, not because they were titled so by emperors or wear red robes or were looked up to by society, but because of their courage to live an ordinary, normal, honest life.

Our father identifies certain individuals as part of his spiritual background. Few of them were teachers. Despite the fact that none of them were involved in religious establishments, most of them are still exalted by oriental religions, even though they lived natural, unadorned lives.

You can find the description of these "teachers" in the *Complete Works of Lao Tzu, Attaining Unlimited Life* (the teachings of Chuang Tzu), and other books our father has written. He considers Lao Tzu, Chuang Tzu, Lieh Tzu, Kou Hong, Chen Tuan and others as models for his own life, his students and his family.

In order to avoid confusion, we will henceforth avoid using the word "Tao." We will serve people with language which is more simple, direct, straightforward and truthful.

Our relationship with "Taoism" ends here and now. The Integral Way serves as a broad spiritual education to all people. We live with the truth which has no contention, no conflict and no struggle. We support our own lives through our own labor. However, our teaching is not what supports our lives; it is our offering to others. We do not take anyone's bread from their plates.

IV

Our father has been in the West for the past fifteen years. His training and cultural background was the ancient spiritual guidance of the subtle essence, as elaborated in the works of Lao Tzu, Chuang Tzu, Lieh Tzu and Wen Tzu, whose works are quoted in his book, *Tao, the Subtle Universal Law and the Integral Way of Life.*

New Taoist teachers and priests who have come to the West use the word Tao, but because Tao was often misrepresented during the 1960s in American society, we prefer phrases like "natural spiritual truth," "integral truth," etc., to avoid further confusion and misunderstanding.

Now we would like to further clarify our teaching.

V

1. Chinese religions, whether Buddhism or Taoism, if done correctly, externalize internal reality. They personify internal energy, and natural energy such as stars, as gods or Buddhas. They do this with literary skill, but such personifications lack scientific accuracy. In our teaching, a student can learn internal spiritual reality through spiritual self-cultivation without having to conform to a religion which presents no truth.

2. In the commercial world, goods are sold through advertising and packaging. The real value of the merchandise is sometimes secondary to its marketing. A shrewd or knowledgeable buyer, however, will look for the most serviceable, valuable merchandise rather than be attracted by beautiful advertisements or packages. Similarly, a serious spiritual student will ignore the decorative wrappings of a teaching and look directly into the real thing.

Instead of being lead astray by the skin-deep attraction and temptation of seductively worded creeds and the beautiful wrappings of ritual, a student of deep nature chooses to directly reach for the direct truth.

3. There are levels of spiritual learning, and religion is at the level of advertising and packaging. In fact, the packaging is the religion; without special training programs that would carry truth and guide students to reach the truth, a religion goes no deeper than superficial belief.

When you pursue spiritual learning, first you see the fence. Then you approach the walls, pass through the door, go down the hall and enter a certain room. That is what oriental methods such as Taoism, Zen Buddhism or Esoteric Buddhism do. These three religions carry approximately the same truth, though they differ in their approaches to training immature students to become mature. All three of these systems usually require a student to spend a lifetime of learning and go through many complicated steps to reach the original simple truth. In other words, they are psychological approaches.

In our teaching, we break down the fence and the walls and construct no doors or halls. We present all people with material that a student can understand. This it is not like the material most religious teachers give, which, if the student is lucky enough, enables one to reach an understanding in this lifetime or many lifetimes later. With our material, a student could in one lifetime discover the truth that is in his own life being, directly with no separation. Whoever is interested can take the detour and enjoy the fence, the walls, the doors, the hall and the corridors with amazing emotions and all kinds of unnecessary complications.

We respect the naturally inspired and developed people of ancient times who experienced different religions and who understood the difference between the religious way and the Integral Way. Because the religious way is a detour that wastes energy, they established a direct way.

4. A natural person consists of a mind, body and soul, thus you need three types of service. There are all types and all levels of service. Some learning programs such as religion can serve you well, but others make you dependent on them like a constant consumer.

In our learning, you are not a customer or traveler who takes a drink that someone gives or sells you from a fountain or a well at the roadside. You become the well or spring. Your thirst is not only satisfied, but you have more than enough to offer other people without damaging or diminishing yourself.   How much benefit can you attain from such achievement? From this you can see the difference between a religion and the value of self-study, which is traditionally termed spiritual self-cultivation.

5. When our father was young, he had some experience of modern education. This is the story he told us about it. He said, "In the second or third grade, the school curriculum had a subject called handcrafts. All students were required to make something such as a kite, a boat, a model house, etc. and bring it to school to be graded. Most parents made the article to help their children get a better grade. When I brought the materials from school, my parents did not help me make it. They would only offer advice if I asked them. Thus, my grades in handcraft were far behind those of my classmates. I felt badly about it, but my mother told me I should be happy because it was my own true handwork. She told me that I was not working just to earn a grade, but to learn what I could really do. Later, I considered this a great illustration for our internal school: to work for reality rather than for external recognition.

He also told us, "On some social occasions, people enjoy playing Ma Jiang. Once in my thirties I visited a family during the Chinese New Year and was invited to play. I knew nothing about Ma Jiang. The family introduced me to the niece of the hostess and requested her to help me play the game. We sat there playing for several hours. She instructed me to pick up certain bone carved pieces and discard others and to organize my hand in a certain way, etc. She acted as my mind, and since it is Chinese custom that people converse while playing the game, I did not know at all what I was doing. I lost some small money but did so with the dignity of a gentleman. I think they were testing me to see if they would accept me. It seems the family wished for me to develop a friendship with the young lady. It was a friendly gathering, but I do not remember anything about the skill or the system of Ma Jiang, because somebody else actually played for me.

Although I looked like a well-trained, skillful player, I was not.
And I learned nothing.

"In China, the game of Ma Jiang is like a religion. For
many people, it is a cure for emotions and reduces the
tension of competition in a man's world, etc. It is only
through practice that the game can actually be learned. I am
using this game only as an illustration; I do not suggest we
learn to play it. Similarly, if you depend upon what preachers
say or writers write, you will not discover spiritual reality, you
will only attain superficial knowledge. You can only achieve
yourself spiritually by practicing spiritual self-cultivation."

VI

Our father was once asked by a student whether the
ancient ones refused to change as the world around them
changed. We feel that his answer to this question would be
helpful to other students as well.

"The subtle essence is the truth. When the ancient
developed ones attained the natural truth as the center of life,
they flowed with the changes of fashion, but they refused to
give up the essence they had already attained in exchange for
anything untruthful fashions. For example, communism became quite attractive to some people in the beginning of this
century. Many people think it is the truth and offer their lives
to it. This political fashion affected certain societies very
strongly, but it has failed in Russia after 74 years. Objectively, it can be considered part of our social evolution, a necessary step for awakening political leaders and people strongly
interested in politics.

"Organized religions are a kind of social fashion that
stunts personal pursuit and research into the nature of life.
Whenever religious thought becomes dominant in a society,
the possibility of spiritual development slows down or stops
altogether, new discoveries and new fashions of thought then
become necessary to break out of the existing religious
dominance.

"Western society has achieved some measure of separation between religion and science. This has made the mind
and spirit go different ways. What we continue - the ancient
discovery - is the achievement of a million years of human

life. It considers the whole universe and each individual life to be models of an energy field. This energy field is not limited to material investigation.

"At the deepest or highest part of this energy field, there is nothing which can be called spiritual or material, because at that point no further discrimination can be made. There was only discrimination of two energies; thus, the ancient wise ones simply used the T'ai Chi symbol to represent the basic organization of the universe as the combination, cooperation or unity of two kinds of force operating together.

"From the basic foundation of those two forces, comes matter and all lives. Life cannot be separated from matter, nor can matter be separated from the entirety of universal life. There are only different levels of balance between the two. Human life is the best model of the true beingness of life: body, mind and spirit form a natural trinity representing universal life.

"Organized religion with its mythology attracts people on the emotional level, and its rituals and customs are easily accepted by a society or community. Religion is a product of the mind, as are different aspects of the social structure such as politics, economics, etc. These creations cannot directly reveal truth, but neither can they escape the subtle law which is a function of the ultimate truth, the T'ai Chi principle.

"You ask if the ancient achieved ones tried to avoid the changes that came to them. They did not. We go through many changes in life; that is external. It is our life essence which experiences external changes.

"Also, some people experience change internally. There is a right change and a wrong change. In the old tradition, we have a book called *Changes*. Its subject is the study of all possible change and the proper way to respond to change. Nobody can expect life not to change or for society to stay the same. However, there is a certain wisdom that can help people see which direction is health and which direction which would cause waste and sacrifice such as an overstrong government, overstrong religion, or overstrong union which would deprive an individual of his or her natural right to know what is right for oneself and for the external world.

"In today's commercial world, it is easy to become a victim of advertising or propaganda. If you do not develop your complete system of mind, spirit and body so that you are able to make the right choice from among all possibilities, you cannot serve your life correctly. You are pulled away by temptation or other forces. Would you like a narrow-minded politician to seize the world? Nobody can develop themselves highly before being born, yet there are principles which need to be learned. All life, whatever age, needs to be equipped with the knowledge of how to make changes and how to adapt to change.

"Our subject is spiritual learning and spiritual teaching. Some people do better with self-cultivation and others do better in group study. We respect both ways. It is because we feel that a flexible principle is more useful than a fossilized teaching. For example, Confucius made a positive cultural contribution, but people codified his teachings. Unfortunately, they become nothing more than dogma to Chinese society.

"If we compare the original teaching of Lao Tzu with folk Taoism, we can see that there is no relationship. 'Taoism' conflicts with Lao Tzu's original teaching rather than serving it. This is why we bear ourselves, our work and our service as a broad spiritual education to people from all spiritual and religious backgrounds and all intellectual levels. We wish that this teaching is never turned into a social tool with which someone can negatively play. We hope that this teaching brings about a change in spiritual education, not only for a few people, but all people. Then a good change will be seen. Businessmen will be more responsible in their commerce and politicians will work for the real benefit of the people to reduce partisanship. Religious leaders will find new life in the old shell of religious teachings and give better and more reasonable service to all generations. All shall move in a new and better direction. A move is a change.

"The question is, did the ancient achieved ones refuse to change superficially? In depth, they enjoyed nature, which offers more variety than human leaders who work toward uniformity and attempt to destroy all variety. When a person of natural truth and simple natural essence enjoys the variety of culture the world offers, he or she does not lose their spiritual essence, wisdom or vision that has been developed through the years. He or she knows the amount and depth of involvement related with change and variety.

"Those businessmen who attain the essence of life will be more responsible. Whether young or old, male or female, those people know what can be commercialized and exchanged for making a living and what cannot be commercialized, such as one's virtue, character and soul. Commercializing one's virtue, character or soul brings harm to other people and oneself."

VII

On another occasion, our father addressed the subject of spiritual achievement and change in more depth, and we present that talk here since it is a topic that is very germane to the lives of everyone living in this age of rapid sociological and technological change.

"The Integral Way is the essential spiritual achievement of the ancient developed ones. It embodies their spiritual achievement. It is on a different level than the social changes which have happened throughout human history.

"Spiritual essence is different than changes in society or in ways of making a living. We have records that show mankind's change in means of making a living. People first relied upon hunting, then herdsmanship, agriculture, industry, and now technology. We shall see more changes in the future and cannot predict what they will be. However, changes are not the spiritual essence of life. The spiritual essence of life is what is applied to different life situations in order to make progress. In other words, changes in the means of life are the result of applying the spiritual essence of life to different things.

"Spiritual energy, the energy contained in human beings, can be increased or decreased in an individual life. The spiritual quality of a person goes through the experience of life and is either refined or suppressed by contamination. Spiritual quality and inclination of mind can be observed in human expressions such as art. Human artistic trends also show the evolution of humanity's spiritual quality and inclination of mind as a whole. What was once primitive is now sophisticated and complex. As the human mind was stimulated by change, artistic expression also changed. Yet, the essence I talk about - the subtle essence - cannot be replaced by any change or any human creation.

"When a human being is born, the body and the mind begin to grow, and so does the spiritual energy. All parents wish for their children to develop exceptionally well, but some develop more than others. Some find the right expression through which to exercise their good qualities, but others are not as lucky.

"The subtle essence functions in the center of the physical body. The individual who cultivates gathers energy and brings it to the center of the body. There are basically two elements that comprise the human mind: one is the subtle substance or subtle essence of life, and the other is a good brain that carries such subtle essence. Everybody has a brain, but the brain is not everything. The brain is a tool. Although the brain is important, it is what is in the brain - the subtle essence - exercising itself through the great tool of brain that brings about anything of importance. The brain is important, but it is useless without the power that fuels it. That power is what I call subtle energy or subtle essence.

"Lao Tzu called the subtle essence Tao, the mother, the 'Wu' (non-being) and the 'Poh' (the plain substance). That subtle essence expresses its quality only through circumstance. Thus, each human life has three parts that express the integral truth. One is the subtle substance of the mind, or the spirits. The second is the substance that carries the subtle essence: the physical brain and the body. Physical life contains the subtle essence. The third part is a field or environment or circumstance of life which lures the application of the other two. The Integralness of spiritual truth cannot be known if one of these three partners is lacking. This is easy to understand.

"Beyond this, you need to consider how to nurture, grow, develop, protect, exercise and apply the subtle essence you carry within you correctly and effectively in the right circumstance. This is important.

"For example, among four people of equal mentality, one will find the right expression, but one will not be lucky enough, one will not be virtuous enough, and one will not be wise enough to apply the gift in a good direction. These different expressions of the natural energy cause some people to be or appear to be good, bad, positive, negative and so forth. At this moment, I am not emphasizing differences between people, but only wish to point out the importance of the subtle essence. My point is that the subtle essence or spirit is the foundation of each person. How one copes with all types of the subtle essence, whether more refined or more coarse, is what determines how the mind is used. The subtle essence contained within a person is also influenced by other factors in life, such as physical health, environmental stimulation, influence and pressure, all of which produce the best mental ability or clarity, etc. At this time, my focus is not the expansion of the mind but to guide you to understand the subtle essence.

"Now let us continue to concentrate on the subtle essence as human spirituality and work further upon understanding what the subtle essence is. The subtle essence is also called "spirit."

"Human spirit is originally the same in all people. Each person who is born has a human spirit similar to other humans. However, the spirit and its expression are shaped by the environment of each person. For example, people who live in different geographical locations, such as islands, ocean coasts, inland plains or deserts, will all be different because the environment assists in shaping an individual's personality and expression. Differences between cultures and religions also arise because of different environmental influences.

"A person who attains the subtle essence is above the influence of environment. This person understands the origin of all religions and customs and considers that to be more important than the religious expressions or spiritual customs themselves. This is even more true at the subtle level of mentality; when one understands the origin of thought, one considers that origin more important than thoughts themselves. Yet, despite its subtlety, thought or mentality is powerful. Mentality may be subtle to people who are unable to see the same final truth of life, but the expression and manifestation of the mind can result in arguments or wars, even though the origin of the thoughts is the subtle essence.

"Only those who have attained knowledge and true vision directly experience the subtle essence, which cannot be limited to any description, definition, terminology, ritual or posture. Because they have embraced the subtle essence, they are able to remain above and beyond all conflicts.

"Before, in my work, I have used the word "Tao" to describe the subtle essence. However, I wonder if it is helpful to use that term because there are so many people who are unfamiliar with it. The expression itself is not important, but I still need to find the best description or closest definition of the subtle essence. For this, the concept of the "Integral Way" is helpful.

"The Integral Way overlooks differences, conflicts and disagreements among different spiritual expressions. The Integral Way uses common words and everyday life experience to help you reach the subtle essence.

"A serious student who learns spiritual reality or the Integral Way need not be bothered by differences in religious expression or terminology because the subtle essence stands behind all of them. In following the Integral Way, it is important to remain open to developing one's own deep vision to see through external appearances, expressions and colorful ornaments to reach the subtle truth.

"The Integral Way developed in China as esoteric teaching among achieved teachers and masters who carried its subtle truth. They were all leaders of different religions, yet they were disinterested in being religious leaders and were devoted instead to the study and cultivation of the essence behind religion. They avoided religion because religion is so interwoven with social skills that it obfuscates the deep spiritual truth. When religious leaders, even those who are developed, adjust their teaching to fit the undeveloped masses, they block their followers' vision of the truth; religions habitually sacrifice truth to meet the common denominator rather than bringing people up to the level of truth.

"In China, there are many different schools of philosophy. Confucianism, Mohism and Taoism all arose at different times in Chinese history, as did the school of Yin and Yang and many schools of Buddhism, which came to China from the South, not to mention the arrival of Christianity, Judaism and Islam. Thus, in China there are as many spiritual expressions and attractions as there are everywhere in the world.

"Each of these schools has something to offer, but there is something greater and broader which contains the essence and truth of all of them. That is the Integral Way, which breaks down all differentiating walls, fences and compartments of religion or philosophy. Without walls and fences, it is possible to reach the subtle essence directly.

"This essence can be expressed in many ways, but it is still difficult for an achieved one to teach or pass its truth to another person. Most religions only allow their students to study or continue their exact expression and terminology or to read only their own holy book. However, since the Integral Way recognizes that all religions are the same, it takes what is most important - the essence - from all holy books and puts the rest aside. This is an important attitude in spiritual learning and is a spiritual achievement as well.

"The Integral Way regards spiritual learning as a journey to the center of a city. There are many streets and different ways one can take to get there. A person also has a choice of many different vehicles such as a car, bus or bicycle, but no matter which way or which vehicle one takes, he or she can still reach the center of the city.

"Attaining the essence of spiritual learning through the Integral Way is like being in the center of the city and having the view of the entire city around you. You can see all the surroundings, with people approaching from many directions. However, most of the people who are arriving only know one way to approach the center of the city, which is the way they came. When they teach that way, therefore, they teach partiality. The Integral Way knows all the ways and all the directions. This is why the teaching of the Integral Way encourages students to be open and allows them to look for what is best for them.

"Truthfully, the most common, ordinary life experiences can guide you to be enlightened by the subtle truth.

"Typically, if a person believes in Jesus, that person cannot also worship Buddha. Or if a person accepts Jehovah as the only name of the spiritual lord, he or she could not also accept Allah or the ritualistic, worship of Islam. Most people limit themselves because their thought patterns have been formed by local customs. Yet, the Integral Way suggests that a person need not follow one way or forsake another. Rather, it believes that the way that works best for you is the most direct way to reach the spiritual essence.

"During different stages of your life and different stages of reaching maturity, you need external things to help you. Thus, it is all right to adopt whatever practices are within your reach to help you grow, but please do not become blocked by them. By this I mean, continue to learn and grow through new experience. An infant uses a cradle as a bed and a place to play. However, once the infant grows, he or she cannot stay in that cradle. To do so would block development and learning.

"If you do not have time to study all religions and no opportunity to enjoy the variety of different colorful customs, an effective study can still be made through my book, *The Esoteric Tao Teh Ching*, which can serve as a tool for personal growth. The other books of our father discuss that same teaching from different angles.

"An experienced teacher of the Integral Way can discuss a subject in a way that can help you learn the truth without deviating from your central subtle essence. Spiritual growth, achievement and development is the purpose of the Integral Way. A teacher of the Integral Way does not necessary hold the *Tao Teh Ching*, which is usually considered the main text of Taoism, as the only practical spiritual book. Most folk Taoists even do not understand it. They keep performing superficial religious rituals and consider themselves to be practicing "true Taoism," even they are unable to recognize the spiritual truth of nature and make it available to their students. Applying a general religious conception like this to the Integral Way will only cause deviation.

"Folk Taoism developed as a religion and offers people an interesting way of worship. By putting gods of different religions into the same temple, they worship the shells instead of reaching the essence behind those shells. In folk Taoism, gods with different names and faces and robes share the same altar. The doctrines of different religions are also put into the same book without true understanding.

"The Integral Way does not rigidly mix or blend different teachings; it takes the essence of all religions or the truth that the achieved ones have reached. It leaves the doors and walls of different religions behind; these are only the external shells. It reaches for the depth of all souls, the common soul - Tao.

"A student of religion may be considered a good follower by virtue of being devoted to one teaching, but a student of the Integral Way is open to the teaching of all who have really achieved themselves spiritually."

VIII

In keeping with the spirit of openness, our father once interpreted Jesus' teaching of "the Sermon on the Mount" in the following verses. Jesus' teaching is written first, and Master Ni's interpretation follows in italics.

Blessed are the poor in spirit,
    for theirs is the kingdom of Heaven.
Blessed are the poor,
    for they shall improve their own lives
    and the lives of others who are also impoverished.

Blessed are those who mourn,
    for they shall be comforted.
Blessed are those who mourn,
    for they shall dry their own tears
    and the tears of others.

Blessed are the meek,
    for they shall inherit the earth.
Blessed are the gentle-natured
    for they shall harmoniously prosper on the earth
    with all others who are gentle.

Blessed are those who hunger and thirst for righteousness,
    for they shall be filled.

Blessed are those who are hungry and thirsty,
   for they shall fill themselves with contentment
   and help others who are also hungry and thirsty.

Blessed are the merciful,
   for they shall obtain mercy.
Blessed are the kind,
   for their kindness will help them prevail
   through the adversities of worldly life.

Blessed are the pure in heart,
   for they shall see God.
Blessed are the pure in heart,
   for they shall nurture their own good souls.

Blessed are the peacemakers,
   for they shall be called sons of God.
Blessed are the people of peace,
   for peace shall support them more than anything.

Blessed are those who are persecuted
      for righteousness' sake,
      for theirs is the kingdom of Heaven.
Blessed are the righteous,
   who suffer from misunderstanding;
   their souls become further refined
   by their fortitude.

This is Jesus' teaching as our father interpreted it for us, and we accept it as part of the Integral Way that helps our growth.

Our father often talked about the misfortune of China. He told us that because the Chinese people did not know how to cope with the new international and internal situation in the last two centuries, communism was rashly accepted. This happened at a time when the Chinese had lost confidence in their own cultural achievement. When the communist party gained a stronghold in China in 1949, it destroyed the ancient culture and way of life which had lasted for many generations. China was thrust into a new fashion without making a careful selection.

The American forefathers who created democracy were highly achieved men. They set a good example for other people, especially the godly models of some renowned statesmen such as Abraham Lincoln, whom our father appreciated greatly. Of Lincoln's piece called the "Ten Cannots." Master Ni said, "If early in this century, the Chinese people had the zeal to study the good teaching of Lincoln, they would not have suffered more than forty years of sacrifice and waste. It is not that the ancient sages of China could not produce such good teaching, but that good teaching always needs new leaders to refresh it for the new generation. If Lincoln's teaching was accepted as readily as the teaching of Marx and Lenin, it would have saved the Chinese people from tragedy, suffering and waste."

Here are the "Ten Cannots" in a slightly reorganized order:

The "Ten Cannots" by Abraham Lincoln

1. *You cannot bring about prosperity by discouraging thrift.*

2. *You cannot keep out of trouble by spending more than your income.*

3. *You cannot establish security on borrowed money.*

4. *You cannot help small men by tearing down big men.*

5. *You cannot strengthen the weak by weakening the strong.*

6. *You cannot lift the wage earner by pulling down the wage payer.*

7. *You cannot help the poor man by destroying the rich.*

8. *You cannot further the brotherhood of man by inciting class hatred.*

9. *You cannot build character and courage by taking away men's initiative and independence.*

*10. You cannot help men permanently by doing for them what
they could and should do for themselves.*

Our father commented that good people could strengthen
themselves by following 1, 2 and 3. He also said that learning
4, 5, 6, and 7 could have prevented the so-called communist
revolution and the misery that it caused. And he said that 8,
9 and 10 are good advice for leaders.

In China there are many good teachings, but no new
teachers have renewed the old valuable and meritorious
teaching. The new generation is tired of the old teaching, but
they have missed its vision and instead became fanatic about
socialistic ideas imported by communism. This is how China
fell prey to the communist movement. Communism was
made into a religion to replace the old teachings in China.
However, one religion for all people is never enough, although
the subtle spiritual essence is one and has no substitute.

Spiritual expression and guidance for each generation
always needs to be renewed. This essence, attitude or
principle is carried by the Integral Way.

In China, young people really do not know much about
Karl Marx's book, *das Capital.* If they studied it along with an
accurate version of history, they would find that it does not
describe the social and economic conditions of the time when
communism came to power. Thus, the book was misapplied.
Marx's work was not the background or condition behind the
Chinese communist revolution.

Basically, the reason that the young people of China
became disillusioned with traditional teachings was because
there was no wise leader who could guide them. Thus, they
turned to communism.

The Integral Way can help save trouble for people of all
backgrounds. This is why it is so valuable. It is not a political movement, but its principles can be applied to politics.

Back to the level of our personal lives, spiritually, we
cannot afford to become blocked by one religion or one teaching. We always need to renew or develop our vision to find
the everlasting subtle essence in each new situation. If we do

not, we would forsake our essence to accept the impact of a new fashion without making a correct selection.

The Integral Way has all of human culture as its background, but most importantly, it holds the essence of life above all life achievements. What our father has presented as the Integral Way is his own conclusion from his self-cultivation, which was accomplished through personal observation and experiment. The Integral Way is therefore the fruit of his spiritual achievement.

The Integral Way, through Master Ni's teaching and writing is useful in learning how to live a healthy life. It comes from his own life experience and is also assimilated from the wisdom of the ancient achieved ones who discovered that the entire universe is but energy. They discovered that pure energy becomes spiritual energy, which the ancients called Heaven, and murky energy becomes matter which can be called body or earth. All life energy in the universe is a combination of both. In human life, each individual contains pure energy (spirit) and murky energy (body); the two energies combined produce the transformable energy of the mind.

The subject of our father's study is life, particularly human life. The ancient achieved ones knew that each human life is a small model of the universe, which is a vast energy field. Each individual is therefore responsible for his or her own life. The true meaning of life does not come from outside oneself, but from how we present ourselves to all life in the environment.

The material energy or material sphere of life has long been the subject or focus of modern scientific research. For the most part, it does not touch upon the subtle sphere of nature and of human life. This is the subject and focus of our father's study. He has proven through his own cultivation that human spiritual or subtle energy can be divided into three levels: spirits of the subtle realm or level of human life, spirits of the physical realm or level of life, and spirits of the mental realm or level of life. Our father's experience of spirits (called "Sen" in Chinese) is not that they are ghost-like monsters who can harm people as described in worldly literature. They are the essence of human life. They are benevolent, not malevolent. Human spirits are produced just like the spirits produced from grains or fruit, through a certain fermentation process, but human spirits are produced in process of a healthy life.

Humans can produce or strengthen their own spirits by the process of self-cultivation. The spirits are connected with life. It has long been known that spirits are the most essential part of life. This ancient knowledge has been misused and abused by religions. The truth of the existence of spirits as the important part of human life is most useful when it is untarnished by immature religious dogma. That is why this old knowledge is now becoming the new frontier of many modern health sciences.

In his books and work, our father does not talk about human spirits alone, but also about all the ancient spiritual practices with which he came in contact and learned. He has sorted out and published the practices that help an individual attain an objective view of life which can in turn serve all lives. These practices were originally the foundation of Chinese medicine, including the type of Chi Kung (Chi Gong) exercise which is taught in our school. In ancient times, Chi Kung was practiced to an extreme and considered magic, because people did not know that the marvelous things which chi can do are only a manifestation of one's own life energy and nothing more than that. In practical applications, the healing miracles performed by Chi Kung are accomplished by people's energy responding to their own process of awakening. There are many of examples of people being cured by the conducting exercises of Chi Kung. Even today in mainland China, without using any medicine, people become well from practicing Chi Kung therapy. This ancient, helpful knowledge can be a boon to modern medicine. How an individual lives affects one's health, and the practice of Chi Kung, or the use of personal energy helps formulate a correct attitude toward personal and social living. It can also help an individual become healthy or strong psychologically, physically and spiritually at the same time. Life is energy; therefore, correct living depends upon correctly and effectively deploying one's energy. The whole matter of life is how to correctly and effectively use energy.

Because of our father's strong intention to learn so that he could teach others, he trained diligently to achieve the highest secrets of the ancient spiritually developed people. He now offers this training and achievement through his books as tools of the knowledge of life for the modern scientific community. In the past, such knowledge was held by a few, but our father wishes to make it available to all people. Its practice, however, is an important achievement which tends to come as the culmination of a lifetime of effort. Its suitability for the general public is therefore not as broad as other types of special knowledge, yet, there are related practices which are suitable to many applications. Some are suitable for older people. Some are suitable for people who have natural purity instead of the bias and prejudice which come as a result of living in society and soaking in the contaminated, polluted cultural environment which breeds poor spirits, poor minds and poor physical health. Using any of these practices to improve one's life and spiritual condition, at whatever level, is never a waste of time, because one's spiritual achievement is carried forward at the time of death. It is not lost.

Our father dedicates his efforts and work toward creating a better environment for realistic spiritual cultivation for all individuals who open themselves to the natural spiritual truth. He hopes that they will give up the religious and cultural conditioning which limits their growth.

Our father mentioned to us that there are two types of attitudes toward spiritual searching. One attitude is to outwardly search for God. The other is to inwardly search for the Self. Both are ineffective and fruitless, because if "God" or "Self" are specific items of existence, they must be subject to the law that any single or collective existence is composed of a group of conditions. This means that for a certain existence to appear, a certain group of conditions must have formed. When that group of conditions changes and disappears, the existence also disappears. Thus, if one were to reach "Self" or "God," it would only be temporary. This is not innate truth of the nature of the universe, which is unchanging and everlasting. Thus, because "God" or "Self" are merely activities of the mind and not the eternal substance, whatever result the mind reaches cannot be considered final truth.

To reiterate, when an idea, intention, desire or emotion, etc., is formed, its expression is supported by a group of conditions. When those conditions change, the idea or emotion etc. no longer functions unless the situation is restructured with similar conditions. Otherwise, the new composition is no more than a new idea, a new emotion, etc. However, although it is important to work with the mind for high spiritual achievement, the mind itself is not the spiritual essence of life.

The mind is the tool of the scholastic establishment. The vast cultural creation of educational institutions and religions is an accumulation of ideas, emotions and visions of some special individuals during certain times of human history. At the popular or mass level, a different version of their achievement has become a custom to society or habit to an individual. In individual life, whoever follows a custom or habit will notice that there is both a benefit and a detriment to it. The dualistic nature of customs is important in daily life, but it is still not the unchangeable, unified spiritual essence. For those who so desire, is possible to transcend the duality and transience of worldly existence to follow a pure spiritual existence. In the human realm, a person who lives a pure, natural spiritual life follows no customs but accepts each situation as a new opportunity for growth and learning. The pure, natural achievement is to reach the essence of life, which is not something which is supported by a group of conditions. It eliminates all possible negative elements, because conditions can be chosen, eliminated, changed, adopted or rejected; they are transient. Nevertheless, the essence is not subject to conditions, and is always in a state of freedom over the possible choice of the conditions of its existence. Here, freedom means progress or achievement.

IX

From the fact that freedom of choice is possible, we can see that there are two levels of life. One level is the part of practical, daily life which is manageable or flexible, for example what type of clothing one wears or what time one gets up in the morning. The other level is the part of practical, daily life which is not flexible or manageable; for example, whether you are a male or female. These are just general examples.   A student of spiritual essence changes what is manageable and works with what is unmanageable in order to achieve a good environment for cultivation.

Before a student becomes achieved spiritually, he or she is just like a beginning student learning to drive a car or sail a boat on the ocean. The student driver or sailor is managed by his or her knowledge and limited skills in using the tool or vehicle, as well as by the circumstances of road conditions, weather, traffic, etc. Similarly, in spiritual learning, a beginning student is managed by his or her own spiritual knowledge and limited skill in using the physical body and life resources. In order to learn spiritually, a student must have a spiritual essence which is strong enough to improve the life or environmental conditions which are manageable and to cope with the conditions which are unmanageable. In that way, the student can produce enough security and safety to enjoy spiritual learning.

Spiritual cultivation of the Integral Way attains the health and strength of the subtle essence within your own individual body. Although the spiritual essence is not conditional, so-called safety, security and enjoyment are the result of a group of conditions and there is no single situation or condition, such as money, weapons, etc., that can guarantee safety.

Spiritual cultivation of the Integral Way supports the health and strength of the subtle essence. This is different from the teaching of previous religious leaders who sentimentally deny all worldly achievement. They became disillusioned when they understood that not only they themselves, but also their worldly achievements, all die. However, to know that one's achievements die and to give up achieving is the result of an inner weakness. Creation is the healthy activity of life. Many religious leaders simply drew a pessimistic conclusion from life; they did not see its full truth.

Master Ni recommends that each person live an effective life. To him, effective living is different than a religious life or a secure life. An effective life builds your power and strength as effective functions of your innermost essence. Please note that there is a correct way to build one's spiritual power and strength and an incorrect way. The correct way is to gently harmonize with one's environment. The incorrect way is to be aggressive, assertive or forceful. Master Ni only advocates the correct way to build one's spiritual strength.

Through spiritual cultivation, the strength of the subtle essence supports your enjoyment of all activities in life rather than dismay or disappointment over what was lost or not achieved. Dismay or disappointment is a sentimental quality of the mind and not an accurate reflection of reality.

Strengthening the subtle essence and attaining the Integral Spirit is our father's teaching. However, learning to have internal spirit is not simply a matter of following a group of formulas or rules or commandments which someone sets up for you. It is a direction, a principle which you can learn to understand and use to actualize an effective life. Effectiveness and responsibility both strengthen one's spiritual essence. Responsible living is the realization of the moral nature of life, which means to live in harmony with one's fellow people.

Many religious leaders promote false morality. Under the guise of helping the poor and weak, their doctrine actually ensures that their followers will remain in a poor and weak condition. The Integral Way supports true morality, which improves your weakness or disadvantage so that you can truthfully help others overcome their weakness and disadvantage. Giving money to charities or alms to the needy helps someone financially in a limited way. In a temporary emergency, it can save a person's life, but just giving money to people over a period of time does not help them learn to take care of themselves. People can become beggars due to misfortune, laziness or lack of motivation. Better than supporting them financially is teaching them how to support themselves. Give a man a fish and you will feed him for a day. Teach a man to fish and you will feed him for a lifetime. The difference between so-called irresponsible morality and responsible morality is just that.

Good parents do not give money to children when they ask for it. This is not because they lack the spirit of giving, but because they know that money should be given only when the time is right, not as a habit. Most parents know this, but when it comes to their religious practice or political affiliations, they lose sight of their correct principles and do not fulfill their inherently responsible moral nature. When religion or politics are incorrectly supported, they cannot function responsibly and correctly.

Religions in the past 2,000 years have played a dominant role in the culture of the world, but they have not taught people individual moral responsibility. The Integral Way guides all people to strengthen themselves by living a healthy, balanced good life. All people need to become spiritually independent. It helps people stand on their own feet and live lives of whole development.

The Integral Way is a non-partial spiritual practice that directly serves all human individuals who have the interest to develop themselves spiritually.

The Integral Way is the remedy for human mistakes caused by the religious domination of society which has created darkness for all people, and for the materialism exalted by the communist movement which has brought about no less darkness and calamity than religious dominance. The shortcoming of narrow religions and of new socio-political movements is the erroneous expression of unhealthy ideology produced by unhealthy, prejudicial minds. Religious idealism, socio-political movements, materialism and technological creations are all examples of irresponsible expansion. Any partial, extreme extension of science, technology or materialism brings about damage to individuals and society alike.

In a natural, healthy society, people have the freedom to choose their religious practice and to be open to higher spiritual education. At the same time, people need not create religions to evade the material obligations of their own lives.

Whether used by a society or an individual, the Integral Way recognizes the completeness of life and the need for exploration and development in different directions without losing the center of good, healthy, balanced people and societies. The Integral Way can also be considered the fruit of all human experience. Wise individuals and leaders of society benefit by consulting the history of the human world.

Integralism is the best representation of the naturalness and genuineness of human life. It expresses the natural health and completeness of human society, the earth's environment and universal nature itself.

People who attain maturity and wisdom do not exalt the extreme of any one direction. From this point, the value of the Integral Way by itself is presented for your scrutiny before you accept it as a philosophy and way of life.

Part II

Essentials of the Integral Way

Adapted by Maoshing Ni and Daoshing Ni according to the teachings of their father, Master Ni, Hua-Ching

Preface

Many times, my brother and I have been asked: What is Tao? What is the Integral Way? Which book of your father's should be read first? What are the most important things to know about spiritual teachings, particularly the teaching of the subtle truth and the reality of the universe? Is there any way in a short hour or two that I can grasp the thousands of years of teachings of ancient natural spiritual development? Most of the time we give an answer which hardly seems satisfactory to those friends who are so eager to learn the natural spiritual truth. However, our spirits were inspired to offer a solution through writing this small book in which we outline the teachings of our father, Master Ni, Hua-Ching, who learned from his father, Master Ni, Yo San. His father learned from his forefathers and teachers, and in this spirit we were motivated to gather what our father has, in gradual stages, transmitted to us.

Many of you - students, readers and friends - who love our father's teaching have been asked similar questions. This book may help you to find satisfactory answers and give proper responses to your friends, before and after they have read our father's work. This book does not attempt to replace his work; it is a sketch or summary for directing people toward fundamental answers to their questions. Thank you.

Your friends,

Daoshing and Maoshing Ni
May 5, 1990

Essentials of the Integral Way

I. *Tao - the subtle reality of nature*

When active, Tao, or the Universal Soul, functions as the vitalizer of the universe. The initial movement of the subtle reality created Heaven and Earth as its two major manifestations. The vitalizer expresses itself in the form of three vital forces: yang or positive energy, yin or negative energy, and neutral. These three forces interact with one another to create all things. Therefore, all things are endowed with positive and negative vital energies and are well balanced by the neutral vital force during the process of their interaction. (From Chapter 42 of the *Tao Teh Ching* by Lao Tzu.)

Lao Tzu, with his inner vision, saw the same process in natural spiritual truth that scientists see today in an atom. An atom is composed of neutrons, protons and electrons, which are the neutral, positive and negative charges, respectively. The ancient achieved sages expressed this truth as T'ai Chi, shown graphically as a diagram with two spheres of yin and yang, which seem to oppose each other but at the same time accomplish each other. T'ai Chi is the law which governs everything in the universe, from the smallest to the largest.

II - *The Universal Soul*

Tao, or the Way of things as they are, is the Universal Soul which is behind the operation of the universe and the transmigration of life. It existed as the great active void long before Heaven and Earth took definite shapes. It is something which can never be created or destroyed. It has existed, is existing and will continue to exist, or be, in its profundity. It is eternal. It transcends time and space; therefore, words fail to qualify it in those terms. It goes beyond mind and matter, yet finds itself manifested in mind and matter. It is in everything and everything is in it. It resides nowhere, but its infinite manifestations are felt or seen everywhere.

The Universal Soul, which is pure, formless, weightless and intangible, pervades the whole universe. Vital Spirit, one aspect of its manifestations, is inherent in everything. The

Universal Soul and Vital Spirit are known by the senses and intuition. The Universal Soul finds its primary manifestation in the form of Vital Spirit, and Vital Spirit serves as a means to perform the multiple functions of the Universal Soul.

This is the totality of natural spiritual truth, or the Way of things as they are. It is esoteric, mysterious, intangible and beyond the description of all human language. It operates through spiritual and physical transformation that touches off a chain reaction of life and death in endless cycles. It is omnipotent and omnipresent. It is changeless and timeless yet continually responds to all change.

III - The Supporter Behind the Myriad Things

Having realized that the Great Spiritual Reality is the evolving power behind all life, and that the Vital Spirit of nature undergoes such transformation as to take the physical form of everything in the universe, it is unthinkable to lose sight of the ultimate virtue of the transmigration of life and the transformation of natural forces. The ultimate virtue inherent in everything is all-inclusive and all embracing. Take the development of Earth, for example. The normal operation of the ultimate benevolence or kindness and sincerity of Heaven enables the essence of yang energy (symbolized by the sun) and yin energy (symbolized by the moon) to interplay and stimulate the normal development of all species of life. Furthermore, the sun and moon shift their positions southward and northward at regular intervals and set the climate in strict accordance with the order and sequence of the four seasons. As a result, everything completes its natural span of life as it should. Moreover, the energies of Water (the moon) and Fire (the sun), which find their origin in the Vital Spirit of the subtle origin of all, interact harmoniously and nourish and enliven all things in the universe. It is not out of anyone's design; it is an expression of the hidden nature of the universe.

Great virtue is the reason why the world has been teeming with all species of life since the beginning of time.

IV - The Most Intelligent of All Living Beings in the Universe

A human being is the most intelligent of all living beings inhabiting the mortal world. He or she is endowed with the wisdom and talent for knowing the true operation of the universe and for understanding the transformation of natural forces. It is not that human beings are born wise and talented; it is the inner development of the human spirit that enables them to become so.

The fundamental principle underlying the operation of the universe, life and the transformation of natural forces is known as Tao, while the function of Tao, observable and discernable, is Teh or virtue. Possessing a thorough understanding of Tao and Teh, one can distinguish right from wrong, distinguish fortune from misfortune and understand the principle underlying their development. Learning this starts you on the path to development.

An individual equipped with such knowledge is capable of developing innate potentials to an extent that natural forces, both physical and spiritual, can be harnessed for self use. For instance, you can cause these natural forces to coalesce and disperse at will to serve your purpose. Achieving complete mastery of your inner self and the outside world causes a spiritual and physical transformation that makes you capable of reigning over all things in the universe and developing skills, vocations and tools for the subsistence of humankind.

V - The Distinction Between Developed People and the Masses

At birth, everyone is endowed with qualities of the Vital Spirit, at which time there is no distinction between developed people and the undeveloped masses, the wise and the foolish. However, with the passing of time, people abandon themselves to the excessive pursuit of carnal pleasure and worldly ambition, thus soiling their bright and pure self-nature, the source of all their potentialities and endowments. How foolish they are to give free rein to their lust for worldly gain and enjoyment, thus rendering their self-nature torpid, sluggish or turbulent, causing unrest, violence or disturbance. This is tantamount to a retreat from the brighter side of the world to a land of the blind where absolute darkness reigns supreme. It is no wonder that most people transmigrate in the sea of life and death through countless incarnations in a type of natural recycling. During their transmigrations, people take bodily forms that are dictated by cumulative positive and negative manifestations of previous incarnations.

In the midst of the ignorant masses, there are enlightened ones who know how to realize their true and pure spiritual nature through self cultivation. They guard themselves against evil or worldly material temptations and damaging lustful desires. They practice meditation with diligence to cleanse their minds of all unhealthy thoughts and desires. They make themselves capable of doing anything at will without committing a breach of propriety. This is the way to achieve true identity with the great spiritual truth. To help improve the spiritual life of the ignorant masses, the enlightened ones take steps to establish spiritual centers where right teachings are provided to awaken them in the hope that they can mend their behavior of their own accord. When enlightened people regain their natural sense of right and wrong, they apply a brake to their worldly lust and self-damaging desires and, instead, offer help to the world. They will live a contented life of high virtue and become capable of doing good for others. Free from mental impurities like worldly entanglements and selfish desires, their minds become as bright, peaceful, calm and pure as a still pond that brightly mirrors passing clouds and birds without the slightest ripple or turbulence. And when the objects of perception pass from this mental pond, no trace of their images are left. In this state of mind, enlightened ones can realize their original self-nature and establish perfect identity with natural spiritual truth. As time passes, they undergo such spiritual transformation as to become sages in the mortal world or Heavenly beings in the subtle realm. They become capable of normalizing the operation of the universe and transforming the natural forces in the interest of all living beings. With great merits thus amassed, they can live as long as eternity itself.

VI - *The Mission of Humankind*

Tao first gave birth to Heaven and Earth, and then to the myriad things, animate and inanimate, among which humans play an important role. As ancient developed people have written, humans unite with Heaven and Earth to form an association of three to support everything in the universe. Humans are the new combination of pre-existing energies of Heaven and Earth. As partners of the universe, humans can carve out their own destiny unaided. They are responsible for contributing to the maintenance of social justice and improvement of natural integrity of individuals. Humans can set their own lives and households in order, thereby contributing positively to maintaining peace and order in the world.

This is the great mission given to humans by the Great Spiritual Nature. Humans are born with carnal worldly desires, the driving force behind their struggle for survival and the development of civilization. Overcoming these desires and contributing to the world is the path of humankind's recovery.

VII - *Sexual Desire*

Sexual desire is inherent in human nature, serving as the means to perpetuate the species and promote internal harmony so that the sacred mission of helping the myriad things can be continued for an indefinite period of time.

Many people misuse their sexual desires by indulging in dreamy ease and debauchery, turning away from virtue and duty to such an extent that they exhaust themselves of the vitality of life. Worst of all, excessive indulgence in sexual activity causes scatteredness of one's energy, leading to crimes and inequities that throw the mortal world into chaos and disease. For this reason, people must stay awake to the fact that sexual desire is primarily intended to perpetuate the human race and bring about their own internal physical harmony. It is not a means for abandoning themselves to sensual excess at the expense of physical and mental health, thus damaging public health and the safety of society. On the contrary, they need to practice moderation in their sexual lives, thereby preserving the vitality of life, both for their own welfare and for the well-being of the world.

The best creative way to transform your sexual energy is to learn spiritual development, refinement of the self for better control and upliftment of your physical being. This will set your foot on the path to spiritual immortality.

VIII - *The Need for Food*

Desire for food is necessary for human survival. When you feel hungry, you need to eat; otherwise, you cannot keep body and soul together. Spiritually aware people tend to choose clean and light food, making vegetables, grains, beans and fruit the main portion of their daily meals. Eat meat and heavy food according to the type of work you do. Unneeded or excessive nutrition is as harmful as malnutrition. For some people, eating becomes an emotional mission. They develop a voracious appetite for delicious food, expensive wine and extravagant living. Daily they enjoy sumptuous feasting and excessive drinking, which damages their organs and drains both their vital energy and financial resources. This fuels endless greed and desires which can lead to embezzlement, theft and other malpractices to replenish diminishing fortunes. Extravagant living characterized by over-consumption not only drains wealth and mental and physical health, but also brings disaster to spouses and children. Therefore, practicing moderation in daily meals will assure a peaceful and contented life, free of troubles and worries.

IX - *The Need for Clothing*

The desire for clothing is also essential to human survival. You must wear clothing for protection against cold and heat, otherwise you cannot keep your body in good health to fulfill your sacred mission of living.

People of spiritual awareness choose natural materials with selective but comfortable styling according to spiritual awareness. Clean, warm and convenient are proper choices. People without a spiritual goal fail to understand this and squander their money on sumptuous clothes. To maintain the habit of luxurious dress and indulge in material desire, they use their lives to make and spend money. People of spiritual purpose do not enjoy extravagant dress or chasing after social fashions.

You will live a contented and peaceful life if you practice moderation in your daily attire.

X - *The Need for Shelter*

People are born with the need for shelter for the sake of their own survival. Without a house to live in, you are exposed to the wild elements of scorching sun, heavy rain, strong wind and devastating storms which are harmful to your mental and physical health.

People of spiritual purpose live in quiet, clean and simple homes rather than in magnificent buildings with luxurious furnishings. They will not let the construction and maintenance of luxurious living quarters exhaust them of their strength. The grave consequences of extravagant and luxurious living are worry, burden, loss, financial drainage and ill health. These setbacks will not happen to people of spiritual discipline. You will live a contented and peaceful life if you practice moderation in choosing your daily living quarters.

XI - *The Desire for Wealth and Fame*

An overly strong desire for wealth and fame is the driving force behind the development of a false sense of power. Competition for wealth and fame should in no way transgress public morality and social justice. However, free competition and equal opportunity help develop people's potentialities which therefore work for the common good.

It is a pity that many people seek to acquire wealth and fame by underhanded means, thus impeding the normal development of society. In other words, they thrive on the misery of others to the total neglect of social justice and public morality. People of spiritual awareness guard themselves against committing or receiving foul play in their earnest striving for a good living, ensuring social justice and public morality at the same time. Experience shows that ill-gotten wealth and fame eventually spells doom for their owners. Worldly gain is limited in its ability to benefit a person's enjoyment or provide security. There are, however, great gains possible in the limitless spiritual realm of eternal life.

XII - The Correct Business Relationship

People who live independently tend to be selfish in life or in business. In doing a job or selling a service, they like to do as little as possible and charge as much as possible, making life too expensive for survival. This situation is created by a chain reaction which is started by some and perpetuated by most people. Doing good work and charging fairly is the practice of people of spiritual awakening. In the short run, you make less; in the long run, you make more. This is one aspect of fulfilling the long-living truth. The long-living truth is natural spiritual truth.

Some businessmen have the attitude that to become rich they need just one customer. This is dangerous for the customer.

Some employees have the attitude that once they are hired they will be well supported and taken care of for their entire lifetime without ever asking themselves whether they are needed or if the job is suitable. All evil businesses find helpers who look for profit without seeing whether their contribution is of any value or not.

XIII - The Natural Obligation of Individuals

It is the natural obligation of each of us to develop ourselves spiritually as well as intellectually and physically. With spiritual growth, you take care of your life and assist others. If everything is in order, you can then consider the natural mission of human beings, which is to perpetuate the human race to become a better species. The mating of man and woman as husband and wife is necessary for the formation of a family and the production of offspring. After a family is established, the natural obligations of all family members need to be clearly defined to ensure their faithful fulfillment. Otherwise, peace and order in a family cannot be maintained.

Section A - The Natural Obligation of Parents

The love of parents for their children finds its origin in the universal soul behind the creation of Heaven, Earth and the myriad things. Children need to be reared with genuine love and great care. They need to be well fed and clothed throughout the four seasons and instructed to behave by the exemplary conduct and oral explanations of their parents. They need to be prevented from going astray and taught to know what is right and wrong. Then they will know how to live with people and manage the problems of life with clarity. It is more important to give children correct education and help them start on the right path of life than to leave a great material fortune for them. To help the world be a safe place for your children and all youngsters in the world, help them grow properly.

In raising children, your own example is important. It does not matter how rich or poor you are, nurture your child's spirit with care. Being poor does not mean that it benefits you to be mean or careless. Nor, if you are rich, should you be indulgent and hire people to raise your children instead of giving your own closeness to them.

Children need to be trained with good habits early, even before they start to walk. Always keep the same reasonable attitude, which means do not be too hot or cold with your affection; give just enough caring for your child. On specific occasions, such as if the child has a minor illness, the mother may erroneously yield to the child's wants and likes. Then when the child gets over the problem, he or she still expects special privileges or treats and becomes fussy when they are withheld. Regulate the amount of attention you give your child. Just like the temperature in a greenhouse, do not be irregular and hurt the young sprout. It is the same in the control of watering; a young plant cannot lack water or be over-watered. If the mother worries about lack of support, she might fail to recognize the harm of too much support or attention.

When you decide to have a child, you need a decent, healthy family environment with the relationship between the man and woman being stable and supportive. It is correct for the parents-to-be to live in a normal situation to expose their lives to normal difficulties and the joy of achievement, big or small. All the positive experiences of adults help to shape the child even before birth.

It is not a good idea to live on welfare or rely on welfare to support children. The parents are saved from some difficulties, but the children's growth will be different spiritually because of that type of support. The type of financial support of the family affects whether the child becomes useless or helpful to the world. Although children's natural energy at birth determines their fortunes, the post-birth environment is responsible for shaping the emotional, psychological, physical and mental patterns of being.

Reasonable discipline is the most valuable thing that can be given. It is much more valuable than coddling or overindulging a child. Over-support only brings forth weaklings. A father and mother's selfish attitudes can push a child to have an uneven personality in later years.

Almost everybody knows they need to create a good family life. However, it is more important to keep developing the family finances or respect for money in a balanced way. This means that we have the need to bring money from outside the home to support the family just as eagles or crows bring food to their families. Above that, we need to make a respectable income. It is not necessary to provide too much money to the children; this would deplete their life strength as adults. Suitable financial support is not offering a fortune to your children, because that fortune can stifle a person's inner drives for good hard work. Too much financial back-up shapes a person's inner being in such a way as to be unable to meet later difficulties. Also, it is a kind of selfishness to give a child only enjoyment and no challenge. Everybody wishes to become rich, but raising children is a different art than making money, and there are certain requirements besides financial support if a parent wishes to raise a child in a healthy way.

Teaching children the tools of proper living and guiding them on the right path of growth and development is the basic requirement of parenthood. Leaving material wealth to undeveloped children is like burdening a new sprout with massive amounts of fertilizer which will only burn its roots and greatly damage its growth and development.

Section B - The Natural Obligation of Husband and Wife

Some people are suited to be married and some are not. Different forms of life are correct for different people. Two individuals of different sex who wish to be married and be the foundation of a family, can live in love and harmony, sharing with each other misery and happiness alike. Husband and wife need to find a goal to follow in their life, and make each other happy and joyful. The home will be set in order if each one fulfills the natural obligations of caring for finances and home without fail. A marriage or connected relationship which can produce positive value in human life can stabilize young people and help them avoid a sexual mess and confused sexual fulfillment, but worldly relationships cannot rely on a marriage contract alone. Both persons need to work for individual spiritual growth and spiritually assist each other. Otherwise, the marriage becomes hollow and has no soul.

Divorce is the modern remedy for marital problems. Many break-ups occur when one partner forces the other to accept personal friends or family members. Excess in anything will bring trouble. It is unwise. A break-up for this kind of reason is a result of immature behavior by adding negative elements which disturb the expected harmony.

Make sure your reason for marriage or divorce is not a momentary emotion. If not abused, divorce can correct an existing mistake or a growing problem. Wise people use the sword of wisdom to cut emotional entanglements so they do not die with unclean psychology or an unhappy heart.

Section C - The Natural Obligation of Brothers and Sisters, and Brothers-In-Law and Sisters-In-Law

Brothers, sisters, brothers-in-law, sisters-in-law and cousins love and help one another as best they can. They stand united by mutual love and interest like the four limbs of a body which are inseparable. Any discord among them will throw the whole family into disorder and chaos. In time of crisis, they extend a helping hand to one another. In time of prosperity, they share alike the fortune of the family. In case of family bickering, they try to resolve their disputes by friendly arbitration.

Some people find spiritual friends outside of their own families closer than blood brothers and sisters. They are not related, but help each other spiritually. They are the genuine brotherhood and sisterhood of the world. Because there is no boundary among spiritual friends, they are related in this big family of the universe.

Section D - The Natural Obligation of a Son or Daughter and His or Her Spouse

If allowed, attend to the comforts of your parents and parents-in-law with unquestioned devotion and sincerity. Bear in mind that you owe your parents a debt of life and repay them for all that they have done. It is still a good custom to inquire after the health of your parents and parents-in-law. Treat them with the same love as you treat yourself or your spouse. Year in and year out, see that your parents or parents-in-law are cheered up, well fed, clothed and their existence comfortable and pleasant.

There are also other elder parents and people who did their duty to nurture all the younger ones. Treat them with respect and kindness as if they were your worldly parents. Can you treat all those older people as kindly as if they were related to you?

Respectfully withdraw from a situation such as one in which your parents abuse you or your in-laws abuse your spouse until the wrong doing is corrected by itself. Never pronounce yourself the educator of all family members and friends, although you may help them by guiding them with your own good example.

Section E - Natural Obligations of Relatives and Kinsmen

Relatives and kinsmen are closely related by blood although they live apart from one another. Hence, among them there need be no discrimination between rich and poor, noble and humble. If life situations permit, they attend wedding ceremonies and funeral services of one another without discrimination. In troubled times, they help one another without discrimination, as best they can.

All people can live and work together in the same world or society in perfect harmony and peace for co-existence and co-prosperity. People of spiritual purpose need to look for spiritual independence from all emotional entanglements. You can learn to maintain internal and external balance in family and social life and to keep your transcendental peace from being obstructed by emotional webs. Your true spiritual kinsmen are people who share your spiritual goals and who are willing to help one another and grow together.

XIV - Public Morality

Spiritual truth is the fountainhead of all life-beings and non-life beings in the universe and therefore it is called the Master of the Universe. While in active operation, natural spiritual reality is manifested in everything that is known by your senses and intuition in the same way as the moon reflects its image upon myriad waters. This is the reason why it is also known as the Father of the Universe or the Universal Soul. The Father of the Universe fills all the space between Heaven and Earth, although, metaphysically speaking, it is something which cannot be qualified in terms of time and space. As offspring of the Universal Father, we take the universe as our home and all the sentient beings, the manifold manifestations of the Universal Father, as our brothers and sisters in spirit. Such being the case, all brothers and sisters in spirit love and respect one another and coordinate their efforts to create good works for the common good. Public morality needs to be strictly observed to ensure peace and order in the world.

Section A - The Spiritual Obligations of the Leading Class
Members of the ruling class need to perform their public functions and administer justice in such a way as to

advance the physical and spiritual welfare of the people, the country and the world. They must be faithful to their public duties and honest in their dealings with people. Furthermore, they need to learn from the spiritual examples of the ancient sages who knew how to properly place the able and worthy in government positions. By so doing, they not only keep government organizations operating smoothly and efficiently, but also set a spiritual model for people of later generations to follow. With every government office properly filled by men and women of talent, ability and moral integrity, the country will embark on the road of unbroken peace and order, coupled with prosperity that is characteristic of the so-called Golden Age recorded in the history of humankind.

Nowadays, many people who have campaigned into responsible positions in society run the government according to their ideological beliefs, placing their egotistical interests above those of the people and the country. They practice deception upon the people for selfish gains and seek to gain undeserved promotions and high government positions by means of flattery and bribery. To expand the sphere of their political and social influence, they evict the able and the worthy from government positions to obtain job placement of their favorites and next of kin. As a result, nepotism, favoritism and mismanagement plague the country and the people. In view of the above, we hope that those irresponsible members of the ruling class will change their ways and be honest in performing public functions and sincere in their dealings with people. It is in the interest of the country and people that the able and worthy are properly placed in appropriate government positions. If necessary, they can retire from public office to make way for those more worthy and able. When one has accomplished many achievements, it is appropriate to step down and let other able persons demonstrate their skills and serve the public.

Section B - Laws and Regulations
Laws and regulations are enacted for the protection of the legal interest of every citizen. Their major function is to

maintain peace and order in society, thus securing freedom against violation. Laws and regulations are enacted with the consent of the general public properly represented in the law-making bodies of the government. They are the instruments by which human rights are protected and justice is administered. Such being the case, all citizens should, for their own good, strictly abide by the laws and regulations thus enacted so that peace and order can be maintained in society.

Above all, there is the subtle law of the universe which is followed by sincere realizers of the Integral Way. Other laws are circumstantial and do not decide the spiritual position of any individual.

Section C - War and Peace

War and disorder are the greatest calamities ever experienced by human beings. As a result of protracted wars and the subsequent social disturbances, many nations fall apart, countless soldiers die and people suffer unbearable misery. During wartime, time-honored political and social institutions often undergo such destructive degeneration that chaos, disorder and a general moral breakdown are brought upon the whole country. In view of this fact, many enlightened leaders are reluctant to go to war, even for valid reasons, because of the untold misery, irreparable damage, and mass killing. War is the great outrage of humankind and a flagrant offence against the universal order.

When invaded by aggressive forces, rulers cannot help but take up arms for the defense of their land and the survival of themselves and their subjects. If war is fought with right cause, neighboring countries will come to give aid. Even Heaven itself will make a common cause with the invaded. With the full support enlisted from Heaven and Man, those who fight a war of resistance will certainly inflict crushing defeats upon the invaders either in defensive or offensive military operations. Hence, it is only a matter of time before the invaders will be brought to their knees.

Past experience shows that any war waged without a just cause will finally end in tragic failure no matter how much advantage was enjoyed by the invading forces at the onset. If the war was not just, the war is the failure and tragedy of blindness. The reason for this lies in the fact that those who wage war without sufficient cause often fail to enlist physical and moral support, both at home and abroad.

Section D - The Broad Good Will of Humanity is More Important than a Narrow Strong Faith in Divinity

Humanity can be misused by immature people to benefit disguised evil. A narrow strong faith in divinity can be the worst mistake. Faith in goodness, beauty and truth, although not defined by particular wording but recognized by the heart, is counted highest among the cardinal virtues of humankind. The practice of confidence in goodness not only applies to an individual's daily activities but also to the management of governments, the development of normal relations among different countries and the harmonious operation of the universe.

If Heaven and Earth perform their functions with faith in goodness, the four seasons will alternate in orderly fashion, thus stimulating the normal development of everything in the universe. Similarly, if the government keeps faith with the public, all laws and regulations can be carried into effect so as to bring peace and order to the country, making it possible for all citizens to live in harmony and prosperity. Similarly, if all family members are sincere in their dealings with one another, there will be no family discord. When each person performs his or her duty with faith in goodness, family life becomes peaceful, harmonious and pleasant. If friends behave toward one another with faith in goodness, there will be no quarrels, disputes or lawsuits among them, and they will live and work together in perfect harmony and peace.

Faith in goodness can foster mutual trust among individuals, communities and nations, bringing peace and order throughout the whole world. It serves as a moral force to reduce personal differences, eliminate racial discriminations and apply a brake to civil strife and international hostilities.

The world has witnessed endless personal disputes and social disturbances, political strife, religious conflicts, civil wars and international hostilities because of mistrust among individuals, discrimination between races and violation of treaty obligations by nations. The world will see no end to trouble and chaos unless mutual trust is established among individuals, communities and the family of nations.

How do individuals, communities and nations break faith with one another, thus involving themselves in endless disputes, strife and bloodshed? The answer to this question lies in the fact that the desire of human beings for wealth and fame knows no bounds. The satisfaction of one desire often engenders another in its wake, thus touching off a chain reaction in the vicious cycle of unnatural competition for wealth and fame. To apply a brake to the operation of this vicious cycle, individuals, communities and nations need to establish mutual trust and understanding essential to the maintenance of world peace and security by being honest in their dealings with one another.

Section E - Universal Love and Human-Heartedness
The greatest adversity experienced is the loneliness, stark poverty and helplessness in which people who are disabled, aged, abandoned and orphaned find themselves. Life is an ordeal to those who suffer from incurable sickness or disease and, worst of all, these people are often neglected or abandoned by their families, relatives and friends. How can humankind, with its strong sense of justice and compassion, remain unmoved by the affliction of fellow people? As discussed earlier, all humankind stems from the Great Spiritual Reality and therefore are sisters and brothers in spirit. As the most intelligent of all species of life, humans are charged with the mission of taking care of myriad things in the universe; in this sense, they are spiritual co-workers. Hence, it is unthinkable that they engage in cutthroat competition for selfish gains.

An ancient saying says that flowers are not always in bloom and the moon waxes and wanes. Similarly, humans go through cycles of misery and happiness, fortune and misfortune during a lifetime. Hence, it is to the mutual advantage of all to render help to one another, especially in times of crisis and distress.

Since we are all spiritual kin, we can learn to take joy in our relations with the rest of the world. Always bear in mind that your own existence, and that of your neighbors, however insignificant they may appear, are necessary threads in weaving the texture of universal life. When viewed from the standpoint of spiritual reality, we are as inseparable and indistinguishable as the four limbs of one body. Injury to one will necessarily have a disastrous effect upon the other. To hurt your neighbor is to cut off your own fingers or to pluck out your own eyes. The happiness of each person depends upon the well-being of all human beings.

The human race is a united living organism, created and operated by the omnipresent and omnipotent spiritual truth. We are members of a single human entity which in turn is an integral part of the divine essence of the Great Spiritual Reality.

For our prosperity and mutual security, we do everything possible to advance the physical and moral welfare of the society as a whole. Coordinated efforts can be made to establish relief agencies for the care of the aged and disabled. Day-care nursery and vocational training centers can be set up for the benefit of neglected children and the unemployed and uneducated. Sanitariums and hospitals can be founded for the sick and poor. This is the way to alleviate the misery of the suffering masses and turn the mortal world into a paradise of everlasting happiness and security. The realization of the above ideals depends much upon the coordinated efforts and pooled financial and other resources of people from all walks of life.

As a student of spiritual truth, one needs to learn the difference between the two great spheres, Pre-Heaven and After-Heaven. Pre-Heaven means spiritual; After-Heaven means physical. The developed one teaches that everyone can be treated as equals; this is the teaching of the Pre-Heaven sphere. However, among people, there are cheats and thieves, as well as those who are irresponsible, mean and demoralized, and others whom you could not accept as friends to join your life and spoil your fruit. This discrimination is called After-Heaven. It is important to understand the distinction between the two spheres.

XV - *One Tree Bears Many Flowers*

The achieved human sages who embrace natural spiritual reality find it hard not to extend their sympathy when they watch human beings degenerate and deviate from the spiritual truth by committing various crimes that endanger themselves and the world they live in. At one time, the Immortals foresaw that if such things were to continue, humans would not only bring ruin upon themselves but would also bring doom for human civilization as a whole. Out of compassion for the ignorant, evil-doing masses, the Immortals revealed that the Universal Soul extends itself to the human realm in the same way the moon casts its many reflections upon the myriad waters. When the waters are rough or different, the reflection of the moon appears altered. This means that there is only one spiritual reality, but the differently reflecting minds of ancient religious leaders described it differently. Thus, the religious expression of universal truth is vastly different in Egypt, Babylon, Greece, old India, Africa, old China and among the Hebrew people. When the mind is not developed, the description of one spiritual truth is hardly accurate. The reality is more important than its description by different minds. If we ignore differences, the reality of unity can be reached. Religious leaders have attempted to carry the message of the Universal Soul at different places and times to people of spiritual potential. Hence, religions came into existence one after another for the enlightenment of all humankind.

Religions, although different from one another in their fundamental tenets, have unfailing appeal to people of varied intelligence and different cultural backgrounds. Unfortunately, the indirect interpretation of the ultimate truth taught by different religions has exercised dominant sway over humankind's spiritual life. Such different concepts have created separation.

Different creeds have much in common with one another in that they are intended to purify the spiritual life of all humankind, thus applying a brake to the lust for carnal pleasure and selfish gain. With rare exception, the founders of these religions led such moral lives as to leave behind them an immortal example to all posterity. The creeds they preached place special emphasis upon the purification of the mind, the love of nature and the normalcy of natural life. However, these religious leaders lost the vision of a naturally balanced life. Sometimes they practiced self-denial and asceticism to such an extent that they wished to sacrifice their own lives for the redress of the cumulative sin of the ignorant masses. Even with the enthusiasm of those leaders, people have no way to achieve identity with the Great Spiritual Truth. In this respect, religious leaders have not done much to help stimulate the normal progress of the universe, the natural transmigration of life and orderly transformation of natural forces.

Followers of the Integral Way

1. Followers of the Integral Way continue the ancient achievements, practice of the Golden Way, single-minded cultivation of cardinal virtues and continued penetration into the principles underlying the formation and function of the myriad things essential to the complete identification with natural spiritual reality. The practice of the three cardinal virtues of wisdom, kindness and bravery involve the fulfillment of virtuous obligations, the practices of loyalty and filial piety, and the principle of fair practice in giving and receiving.

2. Followers of the Integral Way continue the natural spiritual inspiration of the ancient developed ones, learning to return to nature, coupled with the practice of humanity and modesty. The achievement of spiritual void or elasticity through the process of mental purification and non-action are a necessary step toward final identification with spiritual truth.

3. Followers of the Integral Way continue the progress and achievement of transcendental-mindedness through the elimination of sentimental attachment to oneself and the outside world and through purification of the mind by eliminating false and turbulent ideas and other mental impurities. This is the way to keep the mind so clear and bright as to form a unity between spiritual truth and the self nature of the individual.

4. Followers of the Integral Way are willing to integrate earlier religious experiences of the Egyptians, Babylonians, Hebrews, Indians and other peoples by offering daily quiet minutes to absorb the power of God for blessing and mercy with devotion and faith. This results in spiritual identification with Heaven and recognizing the fatherhood of God, the brotherhood and sisterhood of all people, repayment of evil with good, forgiveness and love of one's enemies, the resurrection of the spiritually dead, and the fulfillment of Heaven on Earth.

The Heavenly Kingdom was the religious promotion of a hope extended to another world; however, this concept leaves out the possibility of helping human society. The Pure Land was another religious promotion to extend the hope of a perfect life to another world, but it also omits helping the world. Truthfully, appropriate spiritual service should be rendered impartially to all people. Thus, the true Heavenly Way is not a spiritual escape, but contains the purpose of realizing Heaven in each individual life on earth.

5. Followers of the Integral Way have a broadened spiritual conception of one God. God is not a ruler or ruling class, but is universal, supportive energy. God has no name and all names, no form and all forms. True followers of the Integral Way are honest and forgiving, kind to their neighbors and lenient toward debtors. They help the poor and weak, and fast for spiritual reasons. Five times a day, they make a pilgrimage to their own hearts where God lives. They believe in the omnipotence of God and the divine nature of the universe as well as of the individual self. They do not achieve their faith in one Heaven by aggressive,

assertive or dominant attitudes, nor by violent means. It is
spiritual truth that the purpose is the means, and the
means is the purpose. Thus, kindness, breadth, gentleness
and non-violence are the nature of Heaven. Let each individual and each society have its own growth.

If sages were to stop teaching, people would fall into
confusion and become lost. In the high sphere of spirituality, achievement and communication is totally non-verbal.
However, at the level of daily life, teachers must learn effective communication on both the verbal and non-verbal
levels to help people spiritually, manifesting their kindness
and tolerance. The teachers of the world sometimes have
to speak a great deal to accomplish their work.

6. Followers of the Integral Way get along well with all
differences, but work on their own growth and help those
who are open to them. Like flowers of different branches
born from the same root, all healthy religions find their
origin in natural spiritual reality or Universal Soul. There
is a saying that all roads lead to Rome. Similarly, the ultimate objective of all good creeds is to achieve identification
with natural spiritual reality or the Universal Soul, even
though different means are employed to achieve the same
end. A person can achieve such identification if he or she
is not blocked by the reflection of a particular circumstance
or by any creeds, tenets or practice. Breadth brings flour-
ishing vitality; narrow-minded practices bring dead-end disasters. Correct nutrition of the soul bears fruitful spiritual
progress.

As indicated in the previous paragraphs, natural spiritual reality or the Universal Soul is the guiding power of the
operation of the universe, the transmigration of life and the
transformation and evolution of all natural forces. Hence,
the spiritual qualities inherent in human nature are no
more than the duplication of natural spiritual reality or
Universal Soul. The relationship between natural spiritual
reality and the mind of man is similar to that between the
moon and its reflections in myriad waters. When the waters become calm and smooth, free from waves and rip-
pling, the moon's reflections will be as full and bright as the

moon itself. This is indicative of a state of mind in which you can regain your original self, the perfect being of natural spiritual reality or Universal Soul, or the perception of divine nature or self nature. If your mind clings to false ideas such as selfish gain and carnal pleasure, it is impossible for you to identify with Tao, natural spiritual reality or Universal Soul. When the mind cannot be kept whole and complete, it is the same as turbulent water: the reflection of the moon is like pieces of silver rather than the whole image of the moon.

We can conclude that flowing with the current of the ocean of Life and Death, the original nature of humankind will be so warped and distorted as to bear no resemblance to natural spiritual truth or Universal Soul. This is the reason why all sentient beings, including humankind, have been transmigrating in endless cycles in the mixed channels of life.

To help themselves, those who follow religion can examine their beliefs to see what is untruthful. They can look to the teachings of those more developed than themselves to improve their minds by learning common morality as well as receiving higher spiritual guidance. As they improve the quality of their minds and spirits, they regain their true selves and attain natural spiritual truth. Aside from spiritual cultivation, they practice universal love in such a way that all living beings are treated as brothers and sisters in spirit. This is how to build up the good merits necessary for spiritual identification with natural spiritual truth or Universal Soul. In short, purification of the mortal world depends much upon coordinated efforts of all good, faithful people. A new page will be written in human history when all broad-spirited people coordinate their efforts to lift up different alienating gospels and turn the mortal world into a paradise of everlasting happiness. When this happens, people of different geographical and cultural backgrounds will work and live together in perfect harmony and peace - the realization of the long-cherished ideal, "All people are one family," which is quoted from a spiritual source.

Part III

Respect the Unwritten,
Inaudible Subtle Law

This message from Master Ni was sent by modem for the Seminar sponsored by the College of Tao on September 1 and 2, 1990 at the Shrine of the Eternal Breath of Tao in California.

Dear Teachers and Students in this seminar:

This is a greeting from Ni, Hua-Ching. I am now living in retreat to do my unfinished written teaching. I am happy to hear that the teachers are donating their time, energy and training so that all of you can have a seminar: working together, sharing together and enjoying together. This type of seminar can widen each participant's scope of life as you learn together and come to know each other.

Truthfully, in learning the Integral Way, there is no discrimination between who is senior or junior, or between teacher and student, because spiritual reality is the subtle law and treats each person equally. If you are careful enough to follow the unwritten and inaudible subtle law, you will learn to pay attention in your life to what you overdo and what you do not do enough of. We live in the world, thus we are all affected by human culture and society as it has developed differently from natural life. Many aspects of culture are not necessarily beneficial, yet it seems that some kind of social code is necessary in this sphere of life which has been evolving for several million years.

When people establish an artificial standard for living, it forces us through internal or external pressure to try to meet that standard or social norm. External pressure such as social glamour or vanity, is slowly transformed into internal pressure. Whether it is the external pressure from family or friends, and whether or not that pressure has been internalized, you often do things you do not need to do for your well being or happy life. Your parents, friends or loved ones wish you to achieve as highly as possible, but they may lack the awareness that some things can damage your true life.

To learn the Integral Way is to learn the natural truth. What does that mean at a practical level? To learn spiritual reality is to learn how to choose the right response to whatever appears before you as you proceed through your life. Living in society, our response to the external world becomes almost mechanical because we are driven by the current of human society. Learning the spiritual truth, however, differentiates one from what the majority of people follow and from how they react to the current of external pressure. Once you have achieved maturity emotionally and spiritually, you will not consider many things as pressures, because you will understand that they are unnecessary.

For example, making money is a big issue in modern life. Investing is, in modern times, a correct activity if done prudently, because it helps support life. However, once you enter the world of investments, you are not a winner all the time. Learning the Integral Way is not only accepting the reality that nobody wins all the time; it is also balance. By this I mean, if you start to make investments, the mission of your life in the world is not to constantly play that game. Some people go to extremes, constantly making money from the first time they are able to do so until they draw their last breath. Why do they keep doing that? Because of external pressure. Perhaps they think they need more. Perhaps they wish to do better than other people. In any case, they have forgotten that quantity is not the reality of life.

This is not only the trouble of ordinary people but also of some spiritual teachers as well. Some of them go so far as to own fifty Rolls Royces. The reason is the same: they own more and they think they feel better. Do you think if you own more you will feel better? If you own more, perhaps you do not notice that you are also being owned by more.

Be careful. If you think the teaching of the Integral Way is a rigid practice and to follow it you need to go to a monastery or avoid people, you may not be setting up a life goal of amassment of great material wealth, but you could easily be following slavery of personal disappointment. What is correct? I have mentioned before that nothing should be overdone. Do things in the right amount, to the extent that is helpful to you.

What is important? It is important to find the natural balance between extremes in all aspects of our lives. Some of you have experienced living on a farm. The old way of raising chickens is to let the chickens go everywhere in the barnyard. Not for one minute does a chicken stop searching for and picking up food from the ground. It is a habit. Similarly, most people never find peace; they never know peace in their entire lives. Excitement is what they seek; so they constantly search for new excitement to satisfy them, but there is no satisfaction in their lives.

Real satisfaction is to be what you are naturally in any moment, without any special title, without a great financial report or a long list of debts. Whatever the naturalness of your being is, that is the truth of yourself, on an external level. After you truly come to accept that part of your life, then you can reach for the deeper sphere of life. Whether you were forced into your life situation or chose it, whatever circumstance you happen to be in, it is true knowledge or achievement to stay in it and deal with it. Work with it.

Spiritual reality is the subtle law and the subtle essence. It is behind all people. It is also within all people. It relates to all things, all the world. In the human realm, to attain spiritual truth does not necessarily mean that you are a noble or a great leader, or a powerful person. Nor does attaining spiritual truth necessarily mean that you are religious, even if you hold a high position in a religious hierarchy. It does not matter who you are, the subtle law is behind all of us and the subtle essence is available to all. It really does not matter who you are.

You know, whether a person is noble or common, upper class or lower class, rich or poor, in the matter of overeating, the results are the same. Similarly, in the matter of over-sleeping, over-sexing, over-possessing and so forth, it does not matter who you are, you suffer the same as anybody else if you abuse these aspects of life. People who think they are winning by excessively eating tasty food, having excessive sexual pleasures or owning great quantities of wealth may be gaining something, but they are also losing at the same time in a way that they do not notice. What they win is nothing worthy of their natural being. What they win is unnatural sickness.

It turns out that because world leaders are reaching for things of the physical realm or material goods, they are leaders of this sickness. They do not see the reality of goodness, of truth and of beauty. They live in a sphere which every day is drowning in poisonous waters.

However, you are learning about natural spirituality. You needed to have a little bit of spiritual awakening. That little bit of spiritual awakening you gained came through a course of many lifetimes. The spiritual evolution of a life starts with incarnation in a bacteria or a worm, improving itself lifetime after lifetime to eventually become a formed human being. Then it takes many lifetimes as a human to attain that little bit of spiritual awakening.

What is the importance of spiritual awakening? What is your work? What have you learned? What is the guide in your life? The true guide in your life, even if you think otherwise, is not your beliefs or your prayer. Prayer cannot guide you; it is too limited. You are guided when you are in your quiet hours, slowly and clearly nurturing the spiritual awakening inside. What guides you are the higher spiritual elements within you, which you can nurture and develop during your quiet hours. Slowly and clearly, through the nurturing of your higher spiritual elements, you bring about spiritual awakening inside yourself. This awakening is the special eye that can see the spiritual truth of your entirety. With this eye, you can see to the bottom of things and know their true value in your life.

Life keeps on going; it is a procession. At each moment the situation is different. We always need to guard ourselves from the confusion of external changes. If for one moment we block our attained awakening and follow our ordinary or habitual way of reacting to things, we may fall or have trouble.

It is my wish that all of you who are attending this seminar learn something to assist your cultivation. What you learn is a way to confirm yourself in the process of your spiritual awakening. Spiritual awakening is a spiritual being in itself. The reality of your spiritual being is how powerful your spiritual awakening is. You know things. You know the game. You do not let the game of life trouble you. When you have a spiritual awakening, you can enjoy that which is beyond worldly competition and contention.

I believe you have already understood that I am not talking about the old spiritual way of attaining the goal by living one's life in seclusion. I tell you, living in seclusion is more expensive than anything! If you learn well, you can live in the world, but you will have your own special guidance inside of you rather than having to follow the world's promptings. Naturally, even though we live in the same world - or even live in the same family - the enjoyment or attainment of life is different. Do not be bothered by the world, but continue awakening to keep from being trapped by the world's glamour. Never bend to external or internal pressure or attractions. Achieve the completeness, independence and integration of your spiritual essence.

This is my greeting to all of you. At this time, I am preparing more books to offer you. I am not one of the teachers in the seminar because I think all the teachers are better communicators than myself; my English is far from perfect. Also, I work best when I am in quiet. However, we are in the same place all the time spiritually, because once you learn the Integral Way, you can identify with natural spiritual reality, as I do. We live with the true essence of universal life and we share the same universal soul.

If you were a student in the ancient system, you would go find your teacher and stay with the teacher for many years. After achieving something, if it was your interest, you would become a teacher. A teacher was just like a blacksmith, forming pig iron into tools for agriculture and weapons for self defense. However, these are modern times. In modern times, I do not think that teachers can teach in the same way, setting up a particular situation or circumstance to form, correct, nurture and help a student, because the world no longer provides an independent environment in which a teacher can solely emphasize his influence. I choose to proceed differently with modern students. You do not need to follow me for many years. You do not need to stay in a school for many years to learn something similar to intellectual knowledge which cannot be practically applied, even a little bit, in your life.

All or most of you who attend this seminar were attracted by reading my written teaching. Many of you have already prepared yourself for years before you came to the Shrine. The purpose of your coming to the Shrine of the Eternal Breath of Tao is to confirm what you have learned spiritually from my books. Thus, I now sublimely initiate all of you participating in this seminar as a person of the Integral Way and at the same time, ordain you as a mentor. When you return to your daily life, you can guide yourself, your friends or anyone who recognizes your spiritual quality. When I ordain someone as a teacher, mentor or any other position, it does not mean you receive a special privilege for going to Heaven, or doing what you like to do, like ministers or priests of other religions. There is no special treatment. Each individual, by personal effort, needs to maintain a healthy normalcy of life. There is no exception to this reality.

There are two kinds of teachers. One consists of policemen, courts of law and criminal punishment. Whatever else they are, they are teachers for a certain level of people. You are above that level. You need a different teacher, the second kind, who offers you gentle guidance. Gentle guidance gives you enough for you to work out the details of your healthy life by yourself. Because you receive my ordination, you also become a similar type of teacher and helper. I believe there are many people who can be your students and friends, who need only a gentle teacher to help them a little bit.

I also need to point out the maxim for a spiritually responsible person. When you encounter opportunities for money or sex, you had better think whether to accept or not. Do not think "this is only money" or "this just is a sexual opportunity coming to me, so I should accept it." The same is true of any other advantage.

Another maxim for a spiritual person is that when you face trouble, do not think only about avoiding it or running away. Do not engage in psychological struggle or exaggerated fear and wish to get rid of trouble. Eventually, avoiding it, emotionally struggling with it or running away from it will cause more suffering than if you just deal with it in the first place.

To learn spiritual truth is not like getting the emotional help people obtain from religious sources. The religious way is to ask some spiritual authority to help you after you have made trouble for yourself. The help does not happen, of course.

The learning of spiritual truth is different from the learning of religion. You have to learn to be a spiritually self-responsible person rather than spiritually dependent like the followers of religion. The Subtle Law guides you to avoid the occurrence of trouble. Once you have trouble, you need to face it. Why? Because each individual has low cycles of energy in which there is trouble. It is not necessarily a reflection of the quality or goodness of the person, so do not be ashamed by trouble or suffering or whatever you face, because people have cycles.

The current of society can push you into a corner and you will see if you are spiritually damaged or not. If you are spiritually intact and safe, no matter what happens in your life, you can find a way to be all right. You can accomplish your spiritual completeness and integralness.

At this moment, whether I have met you personally or not, I ordain you as a mentor of others. With this ordination, you can be serious in helping yourself and helping others around you, in formal classes or in the informal ways of daily life.

I do not think the teaching of natural spiritual truth is the patent of my family. It is the business of all of us. It does not establish a privilege but it gives us a direction in which to go forward for boundless life.

I do not worry about people. Some teachers or students worry that I might ordain wrong people who will use the name of this tradition to guide people wrongly, but I am not worried. Why? People need an opportunity to learn, and I believe in the basic good nature of people and know that most will do well. A person who does wrong or guides people wrong will learn what he or she did wrong, because the Subtle Law will cause a corresponding response. There is no exception to this. Wisdom is the fruit. You pay the price for making errors but you learn to become better from it.

There are two kinds of people who are friends of natural spiritual reality. People who pay the price for their own growth are one kind. The second kind of people are the high sages; they pay the price for everybody's growth. For example, my father was persecuted by communism at the age of ninety out of jealousy over his great spiritual example. He knew what would happen, but he never changed his mind, and he never changed or bent himself to any evil force. He paid the price for the growth of people.

My father was persecuted by communism during the ten-year period of the so-called cultural revolution which occurred during the internal political struggle between the extremists and those in power. The direction of the cultural revolution was to attempt to build a society in which there was no other thought than communism and no other god but Mao Tse Tung. The leaders of this mob movement copied the ruling skills of the

Catholic church during the Dark Ages. China has a long history of evil monarchs, one of the most unnatural developments of later human culture to stray from the way of spiritual truth, which is the natural development of mankind. Natural spiritual truth is the teaching of my father, a pure spiritual model with no political involvement.

Sometimes you need to pay the price for the growth of other people in your daily life. In small things, you yield, sacrifice or restrain yourself and pay the price of others' growth. Maybe what you pay for is just your own growth or that of the people related to you. However, no one can think, "Once I follow the Subtle Law, I can take advantage without paying the price." No. You take advantage of effective learning for your growth and you still keep growing, because personal growth is not a matter which is accomplished once and for all. You cannot think, "I have grown, so now I can stop growing." If that were the case, the teaching of this tradition would be just another religious framework.

In real life, in each year and in each period of life, we keep growing. We always need to attain new knowledge, adapt to a new situation and learn the best way to keep our spiritual wholeness without disruption and without being disturbed or pressed down by a life situation. Nobody has special privileges in the learning of spiritual reality. Superficially, some positions in life are high and some positions are low. Some people are bosses, and some people are workers. In reality, the boss does not necessarily enjoy more than the worker. The worker does not necessarily suffer more than the boss. A person on the ground level does not necessarily enjoy less than the one at the top. The type of social status received from being in a high place is an artificial product of society. Spiritual truth, on the other hand, is in reality open, broad and universal.

Whoever learns from the words I give to you is learning the limited expression. The person who goes beyond my words to the inexpressible truth knows the spiritual reality. That person I recognize as my student, the mentor or teacher. You have my blessing and my congratulations for receiving this initiation and ordination, good friends. Thank you.

Now, I assign Maoshing to open your spiritual channel. If you wish to teach or establish a local center for teaching, please contact Frank Gibson at the Center for Taoist Arts in Atlanta,

PO Box 1387, Alpharetta, GA 30239-1387. This Center is an acceptable model. This offer to be a mentor or teacher is good for all participants in all seminars held by the College of Tao.

Thank you for participating in this seminar as a teacher or student to support this awakening. This eternal truth can be passed down to all the generations, to all the people who are ready for it.

Part IV

New Year Dedication
and Message 1992

I
New Years Dedication
March 8, 1992
By Maoshing Ni

New Years is always a time for celebration. Almost 5,000 years ago, the Yellow Emperor, with the help of one of his wise ministers, Da Chiao, an expert at natural cycles, started to use the symbols of the ten Heavenly stems and the twelve Earthly branches to represent the 60 and 360 day cycles. This gave a distinct symbol for each day. It was also the time when the New Year's day was determined. The ritual of the ceremony of New Years is not very important by itself, yet the ceremony carries the spirit of initiative of the universe.

Let us use this occasion to dedicate ourselves to the immortal spirit of all human sages. Their achievement marks the progress made by all mankind, and their kindness has guided and educated us to nurture the same qualities they possess, which are the positive spirit of life. They have lived the life of the universe. Spiritually, they were never focused on self interest alone, but were interested in the benefit of all lives. They were working for a positive healthy direction in which to channel the universal life.

This celebration today, besides being the New Year, is also the open house of the new location of the Union of Tao and Man Traditional Acupuncture Clinic. Natural Medicine was initiated by one of our great ancestors, the Yellow Emperor. We continue the direction of his work by dedicating our practice to the health of all human life.

Today we are also celebrating the open house for the new location of Traditions of Tao. Traditions of Tao offers additional assistance to human health through herbal products.

Further, today is the open house for the Book Department of the Union of Tao and Man, which has also moved to the new location. It has as its goal the restoration of the healthy vision of all humankind. We wish that all people could become healthy enough to return to the universal soul.

Last but not least, this is a celebration and open house for Yo San University. This school was started by an orphan, the grand-teacher Yo San Ni, the father of our teacher Hua-Ching Ni. After searching for many years, Master Yo San Ni achieved himself and then offered his skills to the world. Not only did he offer his own life to serve people, but his spirit also guides his sons, grandsons and all the generations of students of this tradition to make their personal effort and contribution to the world. All helpful energies contribute to realizing his vision of a healthy world and healthy society. Thus, together, we are all working toward finding a cure for all sickness, a treatment for all physical and emotional difficulties and the emergence of healthy leaders who will do good and develop human society.

Of course we are unworthy and inadequate to accomplish such a task, but we follow the words of Lao Tzu, who said, "Because you have kindness, you have enough courage to conquer your own unworthiness and insufficiency." With such courage, we will always have more than enough strength or talent in offering help to other people.

Not only the school, but all this work, was begun by our grandfather, Yo San Ni, and on this occasion we honor him. If we could, we would extend the hard work of all three generations of the Ni family to all humankind to benefit their health and spirit.

Dear friends, we deeply appreciate your support and cooperation. We shall take great advantage of it to work harder for all of us. Grandfather Yo San had time to visit the mountains. After he achieved himself, however, he did not have time to visit the mountains any more. Instead, he dedicated himself for 60 consecutive years to working for the world. Our father, Hua-Ching Ni, started his service at an even younger age. He has always worked. When he was 14 years old he was a worker and a student. Later, he was a worker and a teacher. You could always find him in the clinic, even on Thanksgiving or Christmas. He never took a day of vacation in his whole life, but he does not push our generation, too hard. Instead, he leaves us the freedom to make our own choices about being less busy, medium busy or very busy. Daoshing and I are smarter to choose all of these, as we know that young lives need to have more good times and need to work harder to attain certain achievement in order to serve the world. My father never agreed to anyone's becoming workaholic but for everybody to be dutiful in life. He does not mind facing problems and challenges, because he finds spiritual meaning in everything.

We would like to closely follow the universal initiating spirit of the Yellow Emperor and of all great human ancestors. With your help and encouragement, if we can add one small inch of goodness to your life, we will be very happy, although we always attempt to do more for all people.

Thank you for joining today's celebration, open house and great gathering in the new location. We are always good friends to one another.

II
**New Year Message from Master Ni
Delivered by Daoshing Ni
March 8, 1992**

Be the Monkey or Be the Master of the Monkey

Happy New Year Everyone!

The ancient sages observed the yearly movement of the Heavens and divided the whole cycle into twelve different energy sections called the twelve earthly energy branches which are known in the West as the zodiac. To help people understand and remember the twelve branches of this cycle, the sages symbolized each branch by an animal whose characteristic features represented a different phase of the natural cycle.

The first section of the energy cycle, Tze, was symbolized by the rat. Actually, it should be the beaver, the water animal of the same family which represents strong reproductivity, because Tze - which is the first branch - means water energy. The ancient developed ones recognized that water energy is the first element on earth which brings about life. The order of the rest of the elements are 2) fire, 3) vegetation or wood, 4) metal and 5) earth.

The second energy section of the cycle, Chui, is exemplified by the cow. Actually, it should be the ox, a similar animal of the same family, because Chui is watery earth like a rice paddy. This animal represents the energy produced by meat or grain which supports human life.

The symbol for the third section of energy, Ein, is represented by the tiger or any animal of the cat family. This represents something that grows strong and reaches out. Ein means forest.

The fourth section of the energy cycle, Mao, is represented by a rabbit or hare, which symbolizes a different stage of reproductive force, one which connects more with vegetation. Mao means flowers, agricultural crops and bushes.

A dragon is used to illustrate Chen, the fifth section of energy, because it epitomizes power. This symbol is important, even though no archaeologist has ever dug up any dragon bones. The dragon represents strong energy. In ancient times, the leaders of society were said to have personified this type of energy. This powerful image is found in early British, Egyptian and Chinese literature. It could also be represented by one of the huge ancient animals like the dinosaur. Chen means high land or thick earth.

The sixth section of energy, Sze, is illustrated by the snake, reptile, serpent or amphibian. The dragon is followed by the snake because the dragon is an active energy and the snake is a passive energy. In the twelve symbols of energy, the odd numbers represent yang or aggressive energy and the even numbers represent yin or passive, conservative energy. Sze means weak fire (the sun before high noon).

The seventh energy symbol, Wu, is the strong image of a horse, equivalent in the Western zodiac to the Lion, and representing the strong high cycle of solar energy. Wu means strong fire (the sun at high noon).

The eighth section, Wei, has sometimes been symbolized by the sheep, however, it is better represented as the goat because Wei means high or steep land.

The ninth energy section, Shen, is illustrated by the monkey. The monkey is a relative of the human being.

People are impressed by its exceptional mobility. Shen means flexible or formed metal energy.

The tenth section of the cycle, Yu, is a rooster, hen or chicken. More accurately, it should be a pheasant because of the attractiveness of its beauty.

The chicken was chosen as the tenth symbol because of the daily cycle which was also divided into twelve sections. For a long time, people raised chickens, and at the tenth segment in the daily cycle (between 5:00 and 7:00 in the evening), the chicken always returned to its nest. However, pheasant represents the sexy hour. Yu means the weaker metal energy in which you do not see immediate harm, such as alcohol and sex.

The dog is used to describe Shu, the eleventh segment of time. At the late hour (between 7:00 and 9:00 p.m.) when people are asleep, the dog is trusted to fulfill the duties of protection. A dog does not forsake its duties to its human friends. Shu means frontier.

Hai, the twelfth section is pictured by the swine or pig. At that hour, between 9:00 - 11:00 p.m., there is no light, only dark, and all people are asleep. Nothing is distinguishable, so the hog is suitable to represent this part of energy. Actually, it should be the hippopotamus, because Hai is hidden water energy.

Our early ancestors had all kinds of animals as their fellows in life. Talented people chose specific animals to represent the energies of a day, a year and the 12-year cycle of Jupiter.

We are now entering a Year of the Monkey. In spiritual symbolic language, the word monkey has several implications. First, the monkey represents the mind. Learning to tame the monkey means to start with one's restless nature and go through many internal and external experiences to reach maturity. Maturity is not a matter of age but achievement. Maturity of mind may also be called poised peace. It means overcoming unreasonable and excessive ambition and realistically striving for what you can accomplish appropriately. It also means outgrowing being undisciplined and wild and developing a sense of duty and desire for fulfillment.

This particular allegory has been illustrated in the *Book of Monkey*, a famous novel written over five hundred years ago by a sage. Rich in metaphor, it is the story of an ordinary being on the path to enlightenment. Actually, there are several interpretations of this book, because it can be understood on many levels. There have been many English translations, but most translators do not know the meanings of the metaphors. I have discussed the story briefly in Book II of *8,000 Years of Wisdom.* If I were ambitious, I would write my own version of the *Book of Monkey* which would be more serviceable to people, but my mind is no longer a monkey, so I have given up that ambition. A short description here will give enough basic meanings of the symbol of the monkey.

The second important implication of the monkey is the external environment which accompanies you and is a partner in your life. Sometimes the external environment is rough and restless; the monkey is trouble that you cannot control. It is external and therefore not in your immediate sphere of influence. You may say, "I wish everything was more peaceful." However, when the monkey is peaceful, you learn nothing. When the monkey is restless, you learn a lot and come to know yourself apart from the active monkey. In the end, the monkey gives us many meaningful lessons.

Sometimes the monkey represents your destiny: restless and uncontrollable. Through the practices offered in *The Key to Good Fortune* or *The Heavenly Way*, you can learn to guide your life energy and maintain control over the monkey of your destiny.

In this Year of the Monkey, I would like to bring up some questions for all of you to reflect upon.

Are you still a monkey because your mind cannot find a place to rest? Are you continually searching? Do you always experience dissatisfaction, unfulfillment and disappointment? Have you reached enough maturity to manage your monkey mind? This reflection is directed toward the interior of your life.

Do you know the external monkeys of your destiny or environment? How do you react to your external monkeys?

Are you annoyed or troubled, do you keep fighting, or do you give up and surrender?

If you stand in front of a mirror and make a face, the image in the mirror makes a face back. When you stop acting, the reflection in the mirror also stops. If you are not happy, you will see the monkey make an unhappy face at you, but what you do not realize is that this happens because you are the first one to make an unhappy face. You need to get used to yourself and the monkey making faces at each other all the time.

Your monkey business will not finish until you learn to not be disturbed, shaken or shocked by what you see. You might think that you have overcome the monkey business in your life, but who has really achieved that? Historically, many people, famous or otherwise, were disappointed when monkeys played with them and they decided to run away from the monkeys. However, they discovered that the faster they ran, the closer the monkey followed them. For example, some people choose to be monks or nuns to avoid the external monkeys in their lives, only to discover that the life of a monk or a nun is that of a monkey, but the monkeys are all on chains. Decisions to escape are excuses or psychological substitutes to avoid facing reality. These decisions are only a new version of the same reality of the game of you and the monkey. There can be no reality or gain in your life until you truthfully improve your internal and external monkeys instead of trying to run away. Such improvement is the path of self-cultivation and spiritual development, and I recommend it to you.

For many years I have dedicated myself to teaching self-cultivation and spiritual development. Although I still live in the monkey world, I do not live a monkey life any more. I choose to no longer have impulses and desires, and I also have strict control over my environment and destiny. At least this is my goal toward which my efforts are directed. Internally, there is no monkey; there is life energy. Externally, the cold fact of life is the giant monkey we need to cope with. We all keep trying to live with the monkey.

Lao Tzu gave us the basic principles for how to handle the "monkey business" of life. He said to learn to live with it, not to die for it. As most of us know, there is nothing worth dying for, including possessions, because they have no lasting substance. Your soul is immortal and is important. It is the soul which experiences all changes of life, and it is the intention of all my books to help you fortify your soul.

At this New Year I would like to specifically recommend some books for my new friends, *Stepping Stones for Spiritual Success* and the *Esoteric Tao Teh Ching*. They are also worthy of review by my old friends, because they are about the important unfailing strength of your life. I hope that all the teachings I offer help you transform your monkey into a sage. The word "sage" is not meant to bind you, but to suggest that you be wise, happy and health.

The monkey represents one year in the larger, twelve-year cycle. One metaphor for human life is not enough. Each of the twelve sections of the cycle have their respective meanings.   Some people feel supported by each of the cyclic periods, but others feel differently.

Not all people and not even some people are like monkeys at all times.   Some people emotionally are like a beaten or homeless dog.   When this happens, one of your spiritual ingredients is not developed or is being unreasonable.   No matter what you say or what analysis you apply, that part remains undeveloped and unreasonable.   In order to help an old problem such as this or alleviate the pressure people create for you, I recommend that you do some of the spiritual practices from *The Workbook for Spiritual Development, Eternal Light* and my other books.   They are healthy, useful and trustworthy.   Nobody manipulates you when you do these spiritual practices.   In the future when they have time, Dao and Mao will learn some of these practices and will teach them to all of you.

These practices are not promoted by any religion.   My teaching is a school rather than a religion.   It is a broad spiritual and cultural road which started over 4,000 years ago.   It has maintained itself as a spiritual school during these 2,500 years to avoid the confusing mixture of religions which use the word "Tao," but it is not a confused, controlling religion. The pure purpose of the school is to serve you. You have no obligation whatever to my teaching unless you become a teacher and help me teach. Then you are responsible for your behavior, to ensure that what you bring into your teaching is offered as a public fountain which is manipulated by no one but protected by all.

The Year of the Monkey and all other years are just a cyclic expression. Energywise, each year offers more support for some people than for others. In an individual life, self-cultivation is the most supportive way of life: nurturing your personality and strengthening your spiritual energy can enable you to stand strongly in both good weather and bad. In good times, you are not corrupt. In bad times, you will not think of doing bad or using corrupt means for your own support. This is why I recommend *Stepping Stones for Spiritual Success* and *The Key To Good Fortune* as faithful friends at your side no matter what energy cycle you happen to experience.

Sometimes my other teachings are hard to reach and fulfill by people who are in a low cycle. Therefore, the basics and fundamentals are important above all else.

When I was around 17 years old, I began to use the material which is now in my book, *The Key to Good Fortune*. At that time, I faced all kinds of uncertainty in society. Each mile of my trip, I could not be aware of the hidden dangers. When I was 14 years old, I learned from an achieved master who was well versed in Chinese fortune-telling. He told me that fortune-telling systems are comparative and do not actually tell good or bad. They basically give the structure which tells the possible development of a person's life. He said that what serves you most directly and accurately in fortune-telling is not knowing your fortune, but what you have learned about life and how to conduct your own life well and properly. The power of free will can be exercised to its suitable level, fifty percent. After learning his and several other systems of astrology, I knew definitely that each system can give some information about a person, but no one system can tell everything. There can even be vastly different achievements by different individuals whether they study the same system or different systems.

Some special teachers devoted a lifetime to finding accuracy within a certain system. I have used some of their astrological systems to study the lives of important characters in history or society. What I saw was so marvelously accurate it almost scared me. Nobody can contest the universal, natural system of life which is reflected within each person.

However, each individual can make one's own fortune better or worse. For example, even if predicted in a birth chart, it is not necessary that a person die at a certain age, become financially insolvent or be attacked by misfortune. This change in destiny from the predictions of a birth chart does not come, however, from looking for good fortune through speculation or belief in a religion. What is externally accomplished or done through emotional yearning cannot help you achieve your goal. The change comes through self-cultivation.

In the old society, Chinese people went to famous temples to make large offerings to a famous god or gods. Despite their offerings, their fortune remained the same, although superficially or psychologically it was perhaps covered by the stronger emotion of belief. No true change happened.

I have read material written by some wise people who lived several generations before me. They accomplished a change in fortune through working on and trying to improve themselves. They were not like ordinary people who expected special blessings from some strong spirit, god or goddess. Even if received, such a blessing helps very little. Thus, I learned to have true respect for the particular article called "Tai Shan Kan Yin Pien." It suggests that you can create your own fortune by improving your internal environment through special suggestions, hints, conscious activities and real behavior. By so doing, you can eliminate all evil or dark motives within you. Then your spiritual system naturally becomes healthy and strong, and can enable you to withstand difficulty as strong as a storm if necessary. Surely, you will become stronger than any sick or weak person.

Normally, a person of spiritual health does not know that he is far removed from trouble. Although the naivete and innocence of a spiritually healthy person sometimes causes him or her to fall into the trap of others, with moral insistence and persistence, the trap will fall away by itself or be less damaging to the reality of life.

With a healthy spiritual system, your spiritual awareness also becomes strong, and you become wiser. You do not like to contact possible problems. In a relationship, you do not work totally for your own personal interest, but are a little bit passive and observing, kind and tolerant, because you have become wiser.

"Tai Shan Kan Yin Pien," which is printed in *The Key to Good Fortune,* suggests that it takes three years to form a habit consciously and to be aware of all possible mistakes of negative-mindedness. Normally, people do not really engage in bad behavior, but they make mistakes because they do not guard their mind from extending in a direction that contains a personal defect. If you would like to nurture your sincerity, you might decide to use that article as your personal list for self-inspection. At the beginning, you might read it every day for one week or more, or recite it aloud. Afterwards, you might spend some time at least once a week to review it. After trying for three years to purify yourself, you will be on the way to restoring the health of your soul. God cannot help an ailing soul unless the soul already wishes to adopt an external system, to have deep respect toward itself, and to heal itself.

When I decided to adopt this system to strengthen my young soul, I used to burn some gentle incense in the room when I read it. I did not like many sentences in the article because I liked to do certain things or imagined that I would like to have the freedom someday to do them. However, I knew that it is each person's own business how he forms his own soul, so I worked on understanding and following those suggestions. The first morning, I prayed something like this:

"Dear God, you are my personal God. You also might be the God of the Universe. Yet, I was born with my spiritual self, and I know it must have a source. The source is too big and too deep for a young one to reach. I still consider it a privilege to accept the authority for forming my internal being which will affect my external life. I would like to present my reality to you faithfully each day by writing in a diary or through my secret prayers. I will examine what would harm me or make me dark, and whatever weakens or wounds me. From now on, I am the one who decides how I am going to respond to things.

"Nature gave birth to me. I may have been born in wartime, maybe I was born to be a refugee, but my response will still determine what I will become. I will not allow any external environment to form me. I will form myself under the spiritual light with which Heaven endowed me. I will separate myself from all temporary events, never hesitating to sever any attachment which is inappropriate. I will move closer to you to attain total, complete oneness of my immortal soul with you. The immortal soul has no individuality, yet, I know that individuality is a responsibility which we all have in life. I wish to link the mind of my individual soul with the universal immortal vitality of the universe, from where I have attained my life. For that, I offer my life."

That was the prayer I made after spending a long time observing all types of miseries during the war in China. In my surroundings, I have always kept working on myself, although I could not say that I did it without interruption. I have always kept the habit of self-inspection throughout my long life, although sometimes only on specific occasions. At the beginning, I just formed the habit. Later, it become a natural spiritual flow within me to change my behavior, or to correct an idea, decision or movement.

When I became older, I started teaching and writing books. Those teachings or writings, realistically speaking, were the personal internal communication of my young mind with the immortal soul. At one time, I had the habit of writing down all types of spiritual inspiration. It was a pleasant spiritual flow, which occurred when my spiritual energy was well channelled during my spiritual cultivation. After the cultivation, I wrote down what had come to me. That internal training has become an important source of my teaching and writing. Because of that, when I teach, I do not need to think or plan ahead. I just open the file I deposited in my mind of my own notebooks. It is invisible, but it works better than the storage of any computer that can be displayed on a monitor. This is how I serve society, my own life and anyone close to me. I am not the most ideally successful person in the world, but I feel I am achieving the internal and external model now that I am older. Sometimes I feel the trap of others, but I recover quickly.

Because I was not born with a silver spoon in my mouth, I think I am a suitable person to encourage friends who have similar life experiences. I recommend that they try the formula I prescribed in my teachings, especially "Tai Shan Kan Yin Pien." My own version may offer some spiritual benefit to you, if you are serious about working on yourself. Spiritual growth means to be alive but not be determined by your environment. To be fully alive is decided by your own achievement and spiritual choice.

This is my New Year message to my friends all around the world. Thank you.

Part V

The Meaning of Tao

Q: I have referred to dictionaries and encyclopedias, and find that there is not much explanation about Tao as both a philosophy and a religion. Would you explain the difference between the two?

Master Ni: The Teaching of Tao, which I call the Teaching of the Integral Way, offers a broad spiritual education but does not promote the folk religion of Taoism. I recognize the positive aspects of all religions, yet the Teaching of the Integral Way cannot be narrowed down to the scope of a religion.

The Teaching of the Integral Way began as the spiritual reflection of a few sages around 2,500 years ago. These reflections were eventually written down in several important books. The *Book of Changes and the Unchanging Truth*, which reflected the spiritual awareness and development of the ancient sages was further elucidated and clarified by at least three other schools: the school of Confucius, the school of Mo Tzu and the school of Lao Tzu. These four great sources, plus other related achievements, are the foundation of the Teaching of the Integral Way. All great teachings of different generations blend with the original source to become the Great Teaching of the Integral Way.

Taoism as an existent religion was initiated much later than the original teaching of Integral Way. The religion started through a folk movement, but it applied a social and emotional approach rather than springing from rational search and development which are the tenets of the Teaching of Tao or the Integral Way. Although they are different, the teaching and the religion are often confused or considered to be the same by people who are unfamiliar with them.

The purpose of the Teaching of the Integral Way is to guide people to become cosmic individuals of universal citizenship instead of following the religious orientation toward walls and cages. In my work I recommend spiritual and health practices developed in different generations.

These practices have a certain formality and are designed to integrate your spiritual wholeness as a natural human individual, not damage it.

You are a universal person. People may associate with each other and help each other achieve their spiritual goal. However, one cannot give up one's own rational strength or evade one's own spiritual development. It is only through honest life, earnest work and sincere spiritual cultivation that development comes about. Any other way of interpreting the natural and healthy spiritual goal is a bypath or misunderstanding rather than true spiritual appreciation and identification with all the achieved ones I exalt in my works.

What I teach is interpreted as or also called the Integral Truth. What is the Integral Truth? To make it easier to understand, I will give this example. Hunger is a truth that only you can know. It can be considered an internal truth, yet the corresponding external truth is that there must be food somewhere. The place where hunger and food meet is in a decent way of obtaining and using food. Thus, the Integral Truth describes the place where internal and external truths meet. If something happens to only one side, it cannot be the Integral Truth.

This is a shallow or limited way of describing the Integral Way. In depth, each human life is an integral being which cannot be split apart into components of physical and spiritual. The same is true of the universe itself.

The Integral Way teaches the indispensable truth of life. The goal of teaching the Integral Way is universal citizenship, which can do away with all kinds of war, including those within the family (such as between husband and wife, brother and sister) or between friends. Rather than fight, each practitioner of the Integral Way works on one's own spiritual development. By means of this spiritual development, cooperation and harmony will prevail and we will enjoy Heaven on Earth instead of the idea of an imaginary Heaven somewhere else.

Q: I work with your books. In many places you use the word Tao. It seems that Tao has attracted many Western students as well as modern Chinese students to explore the meaning of

Tao. Since Tao is not knowledge that can be passed from one person to another, it must be a spirit itself which reaches to people who study it. I would like you to give some direction for such a subtle but profound quest.

Master Ni: Tao is a common spiritual pursuit of Chinese scholars and Chinese spiritual people no matter what their ideological background. The attainment of Tao is the goal of spiritual endeavor. It has been a main topic and become the question asked by searchers and students. Although it is non-verbal, a teacher always stimulates students with verbal questions about Tao. The student's answer, whether verbal or non-verbal, always reveals his or her spiritual stage and whether the attainment has been achieved or not.

I have used the words "Integral Truth" to interpret the word Tao, because Tao as the Way or truth cannot be recognized as either objective or subjective. No partial being or thing can explain it. Thus, the reaching of Tao is the simultaneous involvement of the subjective mind and objective reality at the same time and place.   It is indescribable. As both a teacher and a student of Tao, holding onto one way of interpretation does not offer true service. This interpretation of the word Tao is a new attempt.

Another way to accurately express or describe the creative spirit of what I am teaching is to call it the "essence of spiritual liberty." Practically, Tao is the spirit of liberty. It is being in a state where there is no boundary, no limitation and no fixed formality. Nothing finite can explain the great spirit of liberty that is Tao.

Through generations, almost every learned man and woman in the old country studied the ancient spiritual books and then searched within themselves for the ultimate truth. Few writers of those books were able to describe it well. I can understand their difficulty, because I have experienced the same limitation of language in accomplishing my work. The language we use simply fails us. Tao, in its depth, is the natural spiritual truth. To put it simply: it is the spirit of liberty. It is not a formalized religion called Taoism.

After years of spiritual study and cultivation, those who achieved their spiritual learning would proclaim themselves spiritual libertarians. I do not use the word libertarian to mean only freedom of action and thought or only free will, but rather the achievement of spiritual freedom without downfall.

In keeping with the precept of spiritual liberty, it is a shortcoming to use the word "Tao" too rigidly without extending the original meaning. Excessive use of any word will not plant a good seed in the healthy minds of our youth. As a young teacher, I began by using the word Tao to point out the ultimate truth or unadorned natural spiritual truth, but now, in order to provide better understanding, I would like to restore the perception of that word as it was, the ultimate truth. Without correct interpretation, the words Tao or Zen (Zhan or Chan) lead people nowhere.

Let us look even further at the word "Tao." Tao is deeper than general religious connotation. In the word Tao, as I use it, "T" stands for Truth, "A" stands for Above and "O" stands for Oneself. Simply, Tao is the Truth Above Oneself. Also, at the same time, "T" stands for Truth, "A" stands for Among and "O" stands for Ourselves. Such a truth is something which can be attained through keeping alive within oneself the spirit of liberty, that spirit which is liberated from any dogma, idolization or frame, especially the frame of self. Thus, you see that the truth is universal. It is the Truth Among Ourselves, spiritually.

The concept of the self is created through years of experiencing religious customs, education, family life, the environment of one's childhood and other people's responses to you. All of these things create internal barriers, but an individual can break through them to be able to see the truth. The truth is always there. It is always near you, but more than likely you are separated from it by your concepts about yourself. It is your own self-built concepts that block the truth.

The word "Tao" has been misused by later generations, and some overly fervent people even made Tao into a religion. Ritualized religious performance leads to great deviation from the spiritual truth which is the above oneself. The Truth Above Oneself and the Truth Among Ourselves is what my teaching stands for.

Ancient people who achieved themselves by learning the direct spiritual truth did not want to go through religious education or training. They could not fit their own true spiritual nature into the false frame of any religion. Quite simply, they were people who had the spirit of liberty, and who were respected as immortals or shiens. Practically, they were considered magicians, performers of miracles, and healers. More important than their performance, however, was their inexpressible spiritual achievement. Historical records were made of those achieved ones, but the records did not give their complete name, accurate date or place of birth or record of life activities. Fame or no fame, they accomplished their lives and became achieved in natural spiritual truth by following the spirit of liberty. They used their inner power or spiritual capability to help people. They foresaw trouble and guided people away from it. They dispensed herbal medicine and used other ways to cure people's diseases. They were living examples of people of spiritual liberty. They never imposed any ideology or religion upon anyone, but they did have a spiritual direction: endless spiritual development. The achieved ones truly embraced the spirit of universal liberty. They never called themselves gods or goddesses, but their lives were expressions or manifestations of naturalness and the reality of spiritual liberty. This is the power which enabled me to produce books to convey the inexpressible truth of liberty.

Achieved ones are individuals who have found the True Self through the Truth Above Oneself and the Truth Among Ourselves. They have reached spiritual maturity through living a true life and practicing religious teaching through experiment to reach their own correct conclusions.

In China, some people later formed religions and designated these achieved ones as gods or goddesses. Although this religious shell is being restored in China today, it is not the true path and is not the direction of human spiritual development. It has been used in the past as a tool for social domination or psychological support for those suffering from political suppression and dissatisfaction. Religion is truly a divergence from the universal spirit of liberty.

In my work, I have freely used many words such as Tao, Zen, God, Shien, natural spiritual truth, True Mind, the

Integral Way, the plain truth, True Self and the direct path. All describe the spirit of liberty. I am not a teacher of Taoism, and I have never accepted the narrow interpretation of Taoism. Although some people wish me to be a teacher of Taoism, that is their own misconception and misunderstanding. I definitely do not like to accept such emotional demands. I am a teacher of the "universal spiritual essence," and I work for the spiritual development of all people. This states where I am, what I am doing and where I wish to guide you.

Although the means by which people make a living in worldly life has changed since ancient times, the essence of life is still natural. If people insist upon old beliefs and customs, they only become obstacles for our next steps forward. If people have learned wisely, they are not attached to one expression or another. A wise person does not hold onto any one way of growth. The way of growth represented by my work is not limited to any single expression; it includes all good, usable, decent ways. Openness of spirit is called Tao; it is the expression of the spirit of liberty. I also do not reject anyone who has religious beliefs or has used religious discipline to help strengthen their lives.

People who attach themselves to any great faith, religion or doctrine and lose their spirit of openness will stumble as they try to move forward in life. You see, it is more important to hold onto the spirit of liberty than to the shell of conceptual ideology or even the physical shape of life. I use the word "Tao" with flexibility in order to carry you to the spirit of liberty. In that way, you can enjoy the vastness, profundity and limitlessness of the spiritual universe.

I denounce the conventional dogmatic interpretation of Tao as a religion or anything that hinders people's progress. The purpose of this statement is to clearly show the position of my teaching. There is not the slightest association or connection between my promotion and the religious type of Taoism in China after the second century. Thus, there should not be any confusing or mistaking my work as religious Taoism in China or abroad. I objectively discuss or introduce the valuable, effective spiritual practices of the ancient achieved ones with a scientific approach. The practices themselves have great value as a contribution to people of any generation and racial background.

Because human growth, including spiritual growth, is accomplished step-by-step, the discussion of religion is helpful to assist one's inner vision for spiritual growth before reaching spiritual maturity. This is true of an individual as well as society. Therefore, such discussion is necessary. I myself do not disrespect it or wish to stop people from participating in such discussion. The goal of my work is to help people's spiritual development. Surely there is a difference between spiritual development and merely allowing emotional reliance or dependence, which all conventional religions have done in the past as well as present.

I foresee all people using their religious foundation for far-reaching growth rather than for spiritual and psychological immaturity that build ideological castles for conceptual wars. I have recommended some spiritual practices to some of my friends. All spiritual practices are a type of communication which carries something unreachable by language which is far behind formality. It is valuable for all people to have their own spiritual practice in one way or another. Most people have an obstacle to going below the surface of religious belief structures. If they stay on the surface, spiritual practices bring no benefit for their spiritual achievement.

Throughout my life, I have embraced the spirit of liberty. The spirit of liberty is what rejuvenates my spirit of life and the spirit of life of all my friends.

Part VI

The Self-Study Program
and Correspondence Course
of the College of Tao

*"If a piece of jade is not cut, chiseled and polished,
it is a piece of useless stone."*

Introduction to the Study Program

Each individual life is an integral being which cannot be split into what is spiritual and what is physical. The same is true of the universe. The Integral Truth is what teaches this indispensable truth of life.

The teaching of the Integral Way is the fruit of the spiritual development of millions of years of human life experience. This broad spiritual education is not an organized type of religion or a monastic lifestyle, but an advanced spiritual school with truthful, scientific spiritual knowledge. Spiritual knowledge is more subtle and not as substantial as physical science. It is closely connected with health sciences, which cannot be studied by modern anatomy, chemistry or biochemistry. It has its own special value in assisting the health of the human world. Reaching a thorough understanding of such absolute subtle truth requires time. The universe is the campus of this ancient school of the subtle truth. It is a school without boundaries, but infinity marks its traceless boundary. The spirit of the College is to attain spiritual independence and return to the original nature and joy of natural life by truthful training and knowledge.

1. Good spiritual learning promotes self-understanding, reflection upon one's life and environment, and the application of this knowledge in life. Its goal is to achieve maturity with fewer mistakes.

Physically, spiritual learning develops one's health through principles of good diet, nutrition, exercise, sleep, etc.

as well as stability in one's life for financial self-sufficiency. Mentally, it is learning the difference between religion and spirituality, clearing away misconceptions and wrong thinking, and acquiring necessary knowledge to deepen one's understanding of life. Socially, it is harmony in personal and business relationships and going beyond the limitations of self to extend virtuous service to society and the world. Spiritually, it is the attainment of spiritual immortality. All together, this is called learning the Integral Way.

2. *Generally, all of this can be learned in three stages.*

These stages cannot actually be measured; they are levels of spirituality with deeper vision and more truthful personal development.

The first stage is intellectual learning, which includes one's life experience and the study of spiritual books.

The second stage is realizing the things you learned from the first stage as the reality of your own life. The best way to do this is through virtuous fulfillment or service to the world.

The third stage is esoteric spiritual practices and spiritual realization. This stage requires the total fulfillment of the prior two stages in order for it to be fruitful and is not achieved by everyone.

These three stages are not mutually exclusive of each other. In other words, for some people, it is possible to fulfill all three at one time.

3. *The Three Stages of Spiritual Achievement: Learning, Realization and Ascension*

A.   In the first comprehensive stage, you accomplish and experience the primary level of spiritual achievement, which is knowledge and learning (See Chapter 1).

B.   After you have learned the material and accomplished an understanding of the first stage, it is time to realize and apply this understanding to life.   The middle level of spiritual achievement is the level of Integral Spiritual Realization. Being a person of spiritual cultivation, you now use whatever you have learned by concentrating more on virtuous fulfillment or service to the world.   This stage spans different lengths of time and takes different forms depending upon the individual. Some people become teachers, but there are other forms of service. (See Chapter 2). During this stage, a person refines and polishes him or her self and thus becomes prepared for the third stage of spiritual attainment, which is ascension.

C.   The third stage of achievement is purely spiritual. It is a different level of life and is attained only through a lifetime of devoted effort and cultivation. Because it occurs on levels or dimensions that are invisible and inaudible to the ordinary human structure, it can be taught to few people. Reaching this level is the fruit of many lifetimes of cultivation. (See Chapter 3).

4. You might like the College of Tao to help you accomplish the three stages of achievement. The teaching of the Integral Way can serve you directly and assist your personal growth. It can be adjusted to fit each individual student.
   One of the main functions of this program is for people to help themselves without waiting for a powerful leader or teacher to descend abruptly from the sky or expecting a messiah from outer space.   Internal growth and truth is encouraged so that the truth innate in all of our lives can be realized.
   Merely reading books is not enough for self-actualization. You also need to improve your personal internal energy by doing the practices in the books. The self-study program is designed to help students who are interested in attaining the Integral Way in their lives.   The program is flexible and accommodates different interests and levels of individual students.

5.   Like the ancient type of teaching which had no fixed plan, this program is also open minded. Students have free choice and flexibility.
   To fulfill the first stage of the study of the Integral Way of Life and learning, the Five Levels of learning the Integral Way

of Life described in the following sections provide a guideline for learning the materials of the Integral Way.

To fulfill the second stage, that of realization and service, the College of Tao offers a program for those who offer selfless service through teaching the Arts of Integral Life.

To fulfill the third stage, that of Internal Alchemy, the College of Tao's seminars may be related to the practice. Most instruction is already in Master Ni's books.

The purpose of this self-study program is to assist all aspects of one's life. Aside from spiritual education which is subtle, there are four goals that one should try to achieve. These four goals are necessary for all individual life: 1) wisdom, 2) virtue, 3) power and 4) happiness. Happiness is the fruit or result of attaining the first three goals.

1) Wisdom: Public education does not teach wisdom. General religious education often confuses wisdom with factual learning. Both public and religious education may cause an imbalance in one's personality rather than guide a person to become wise, so the first goal of the Integral Way of Life is that a person must live with wisdom. Otherwise, the happiness the person creates may cause trouble.

2) Virtue: A virtuous person may not necessarily bring good to others, but at least he or she is upright, self-disciplined and self-controlled. Such a person never becomes harmful to one's own life or to anybody else in their surroundings. The ancient concept uses the word "Teh" to describe virtue. Some sages elucidate the word Teh as gain, because in our daily life, whatever good is done for ourselves or others is a spiritual gain. Spiritual gain will make you happy. Positive, creative, productive, effective thoughts or behaviors are virtuous and will allow you to gain some internal spiritual benefit. A selfish person only thinks about oneself, and becomes inconsiderate and harmful to others. What gain is there in this?

3) Power: This kind of power does not mean magical power, political power or great financial power. It means the strength of your health, including your mind, emotions and

physical body, which can enable you to accomplish a big thing or a small thing properly. This kind of power means being able to enjoy a healthy being and happy life. Also, becoming a useful, serviceable, self-contained and self-controlled personality are all included in the correct concept of power. It means the positive power of a natural life.

4) Happiness: By attaining the wisdom, virtue and power described above, you will be a happy person. Your happiness will have no defect. In English, the four virtues are wisdom, virtue, power and happiness, which are pronounced Zhi, Teh, Lih and Leh in Chinese. These are four corner-stones of life.

To learn the Integral Way, you may read and study Master Ni's books on your own or in a study group, learn movements from Master Ni's videotapes, attend classes at the College of Tao and affiliated centers, or complete the Certificate Program which is also our Correspondence Course. The details of the program established by the College of Tao that can assist you to develop spiritually are outlined in the following chapters.

Books and videotapes may be obtained by using the order form at the back of this book or through your local bookstore.

For information on classes at the College of Tao or affiliated centers, write the College of Tao, 1314 Second Street Suite A, Santa Monica, CA 90401. Be sure to specify in which part of the country you will be able to attend classes.

Chapter 1:
The First Stage of Spiritual Achievement: Learning

This program of learning is for those individuals interested in studying directly under the guidance of the College. It is for students who wish to dedicate some time to study on their own. Each Level is part of the learning process.

Levels of Study in the Certificate Program
of the College of Tao

Granting of Levels
Levels are recognized through the College of Tao. The length of time a student spends completing the material for each Level depends upon the student. Although you decide your own study speed, be thorough enough to make your learning truly beneficial. A period of two years is suggested to complete each Level. Some may progress faster.

1. If you would like to have a certificate after course completion, you must complete the following:

A) Register with the College by writing a letter of intent specifying the Level you are seeking, a description of your general background and some personal details. Mail the letter to the College of Tao, Attention: Certificate Program/Correspondence Course, 1314 Second Street, Suite A, Santa Monica, CA 90401.

B) After you have completed the study course for the Level, submit a one page report and be precise, without extraneous language, about what you have studied and learned through self-evaluation and send it to the College with your letter and a small or large donation (as you value it). A one-page book report must be submitted for each book completed.

The letter and reports will be the basis used to determine granting the certificate of completion. The certificate signifies self-study and personal growth or learning. Those who wish will receive a "Certificate of Completion" for that Level. When your letter is received, the College will also put your name on the mailing list for its activities.

2. Those who have already studied Master Ni's work for certain years can apply for a prior learning assessment and obtain a "Certificate of Completion" for any Level by first reviewing the books to make better use of them. Make a report to the College, and the College will respond to your interest. Submit the letter, reports and donation as explained above.

Those who have helped Master Ni's literary work may also consider obtaining a Level after reviewing the books and making a report. Some teachers and mentors who have helped Master Ni offer service to society can also obtain a Level after reviewing the books and making a report. Submit the letter, reports and donation as explained above.

3. Generally, it is suggested that a student spend about two years to complete each Level. However, the time is flexible according to the student's ability to fulfill the requirements adequately. He/she can then apply for the "Certificate of Completion" for that Level. The College will evaluate his/her report and make recommendations for the next Level of study.

After the second Level has been completed, and the student sends in the self-evaluation report about his/her learning, study and fulfillment, the student must mail back the certificate given at the completion of the first Level. If the College approves the second Level, it will imprint the certificate with a new spiritual chop (red imprint of Chinese calligraphy) and date it. When the five Levels are totally finished, there will be five chops on the certificate. This has spiritual significance and value for the student and may be kept as a personal spiritual keepsake or treasure.

4. Students who have completed all five Levels and are considered eligible to attend special classes of higher esoteric spiritual practices given by the College will be notified by

special letter. Those practices are not for social promotion but are the reward for individual progress.

Preliminary Study

Some students may need an adjustment period in which they simply go through some of the material. This preliminary stage would come before students understand or really become interested in the graded study. It can help prepare a student to follow the grading program. It allows time for a student to seriously prepare oneself.

Students can either directly start the new course of study or spend a preliminary stage of several months randomly reading Master Ni's books. The books may be obtained by using the order form in the back of this book or through your local bookstore.

Most people who have read several of Master Ni's books on their own and are familiar with some of the concepts and terms have already accomplished this preliminary study. Students who have already seriously studied and absorbed some of Master Ni's books can chart their study map accordingly. Therefore, without slowing down the process, they can apply their previous knowledge toward the suggested Level.

The Five Levels of Independent Learning

The College offers a self-study program for those who use Master Ni's materials (books) to learn natural life sciences. Five Levels are offered. The step-by-step guidelines of the program offer general life guidance for all sincere readers.

The Five Levels offered are an expression of the spiritual and virtuous conditions of an individual and do not relate to any specific test or skill. Different skills can be a tool for making a living, but skills are not the purpose of life. One builds his or her spiritual character for oneself, not for other people. A person who handles oneself well will be less of a problem or burden for the world.

There is no time limitation set for fulfilling the requirements for each Level. Following correct study and self evaluation, a student can apply for acknowledgement of a Level. The Levels are as follows:

1) Gold Level of Learning the Integral Way of Life
2) Diamond Level of Learning the Integral Way of Life
3) Crystal Level of Learning the Integral Way of Life
4) Pearl Level of Learning the Integral Way of Life
5) Jade Level of Learning the Integral Way of Life

Traditional Understanding of the Five Levels

1. To realize the Gold Level represents the achievement of understanding or the preparation for attaining the Golden Immortal Medicine.

2. To realize the Diamond Level represents the achievement of understanding or the preparation for attaining the Diamond Practice.

3. To realize the Crystal Level represents the attainment of a crystal clear mind.

4. To realize the Pearl Level represents the achievement of the Mystical Pearl.

5. To realize the Jade Level represents attaining the experience of personal divine nature, the authority of personal spiritual fate. It is a result of the convergence of personal spiritual essence as the Jade Emperor, or attaining the Integral Truth or the Natural Spiritual Truth. (For the spiritual reality of the Jade Emperor, please see the book *Tao, The Subtle Universal Law.*) This book is studied early in the learning, but integrating the truth of life comes later. Such achievement is not merely conceptual.

The usefulness of the self-study program is not only intellectual, it can also bring a higher quality of living.

These Levels are milestones that can be used to help you understand how much you have learned. They are internal, spiritual "scores." The Levels do not provide a hierarchical rank because Levels of Natural Integral Life are recognized by oneself as different stages of one's spiritual learning and are essential parts that make up the whole.

A Level is not obtained by spending large sums of money, handling your teachers well or by great social communication skills. It is obtained by self-improvement. When your negativity is watched and corrected by yourself, your true sweet essence will find opportunities to manifest to those who have the same purpose of finding Heaven and paradise in life.

Group Study

Some people benefit from group study rather than individual study. Study groups may be formed in affiliated centers and by non-affiliated groups of individuals. However, even in group study, the spirit of independent self-study should be nurtured, valued and respected.

Group study is study activity among friends or a family. Any small number of people who would like to work together to share their own experiences, questions and understandings with the purpose of mutual help and benefit may form a group. There should be no charge involved nor is there need for special approval from the College. These groups are intended for self-help, and do not need a formal teacher or leader. At most, one of the group members will need to coordinate or organize. The members of the group should respect and love each other and help alleviate any negative competition among each other.

Group activities could lead to a new way of life as people live together, learn together and grow together in the world to help each other attain happiness in life. One of the goals of self-study is live a happy, harmonious and fulfilling natural life without pulling away from others.

In the group, students should concentrate on their own problems and try to progress on their own. There is no reason for competition, because each individual has a different problem. If, in the same group, everyone has the same problem, the ones who have not improved themselves can learn from those who do better. Once a sage said, "If three people are walking together, I can find my teacher in one of the other two." This is not competition. Sincere students will first bring benefit to themselves and then offer their influence to others. That is not emotional competition.

The College also does not worry about people being competitive in a positive direction. If people are competitive for a good thing, it is still valuable. They will still have self-respect. Problems arise when people are sloppy, inert or unmotivated. Even if someone starts with competition, after gaining more knowledge, he or she can slow down to become deeper and deeper. All people start at a shallow, surface level, but become deeper and deeper in an eventual, natural process. Real spiritual development is not competitive.

In these study groups, there is no formal teacher or class. The meetings can be held once a week. The purpose of the meeting is mutual help to unify the understanding of written material and practices. In the study groups, questions can be discussed to shed new light on personal attainment. Students can find help and answers to spiritual or conceptual problems, personal problems or difficulties from other students in the group.

While each study group is independent, communication among different study groups is encouraged so that the problems and questions of one group that cannot be solved can be helped by another group. Each member of the study group has an equal right. In practical matters, the decisions reached by joint objective effort is valued to help decide what is to be done in the process of learning. Group members study the books chosen by the group. Each person can keep a notebook or diary of personal experiences, inspirations and learning.

By participating in a study group, you begin to understand and respect differences among people. By your own management, learn to smooth conflicts you have with others. Develop your approach so that you can clearly communicate with good manners. In group activity, learn not to have your feelings hurt by others, also remember not to hurt others. When you consider that other people's reactions to you are mirror-like reflections of your thoughts and behavior, you have the key to making progress and growth in yourself. Let the responses of other people help you understand what you do that is incorrect. Look to see what part of your behavior is not welcomed or accepted by others and make necessary improvements. If you write down your psychological problems or self complaints in a journal, you have the opportunity to review them and work to correct them.

Be financially self-responsible in your life. Choose to use money wisely and correctly. Use your financial strength to help set up a center or a study group if it is your interest.

Some study groups start out small and immature, and over the years they mature in their level of learning and spirituality. Close friendships are often formed.

If you are interested in finding out if there is an existing group in your area, you may contact the College of Tao, 1314 Second Street Suite A, Los Angeles, CA 90401.

If you are interested in group study, you may form a study group yourself. It is an opportunity for service and further learning. The successful organization of a study group requires patience, tolerance and working on details to arrange an environment with an open and healthy atmosphere for a group of people to grow together, share experience and maintain an open door for others to share in the development of the group. The growth and success of the discussion group by all participants is dependent upon nurturing the group and avoiding difficulties which may arise by anyone's immature attitude or personality. For further detailed information on how to establish a study group in your area, please contact the Center for Taoist Arts, PO Box 1389, Alpharetta, GA 30239-1389.

Goals and Requirements
For the Five Levels of the Integral Way of Life

The Gold Level of the Integral Way of Life
1. The Goal: The Gold Level student searches for the answer to whether the true value of life is internal or external. Internal means life energy, intelligence, virtue, etc. External means money, fame, social position, material possessions, etc. If it is internal, what is our potential? Should we use the internal to support the external search or should we use the

external to support internal accomplishment? On this level, internal accomplishment means good vitality, clear intelligence, healthy, high spirit and a good virtuous condition. Is there a way to avoid becoming a failure in one's internal and external life?

2. The Requirement: Spend a length of time reading Master Ni's books. You also need to find the answers to your own questions by yourself. You may or may not find the answers, but in this stage, put yourself on the right path by studying your own life. Avoid blindly accepting what the books say. Accept what you understand from your own life experience, and keep the parts you do not understand for the future. For your intellectual and psychological growth and understanding, test or experiment with what is said in the books. You can use the books as your friends by presenting any argument to yourself until you reach the balance, reasonableness and maturity that you can achieve at this level.

In other words, to receive the Gold Level of the Integral Way of Life you start to know the value of life and respect the value of your own life. You start to read and take advice from good books. Absorb some of it. To sum up, you find your direction and a general understanding. By participating in study groups, you begin to understand and respect differences among people.

3. Study materials for the Gold Level:
Stepping Stones for Spiritual Success (The Key Book)
Golden Message
The Key to Good Fortune
Spiritual Messages from a Buffalo Rider
The Complete Works of Lao Tzu
8,000 Years of Wisdom, Book I
8,000 Years of Wisdom, Book II
Attune Your Body with Dao-In

Select the spiritual practices that fit you best and apply them.
The Eight Treasures exercise tape and Dao-in are highly suggested as study activities. A student can also select Trinity style T'ai Chi Chuan and Crane Style Chi Gong (Chi

Kung) for general health or specific physical problems to fulfill the requirement of exercise which is important.

Books and videotapes may be obtained directly by using the order forms in the back of this book or through your local bookstore.

The Diamond Level of the Integral Way of Life

1. The Goal: The Diamond Level student comes to the point of knowing that life is both internal and external. What is the most essential guideline we need to live up to at this level? What is the most supportive spiritual practice which is simple and effective, and supports both aspects of our life being, internal and external? This may sound similar to the goal of the Gold Level, yet you are progressing.

2. The Requirement: Arrange your life in an effective way. Manage your psychology in a simple way. Do your spiritual practice in a simple and helpful way. Strengthen yourself by what you study and through your cultivation. In your job or other place of service, willingly give more than required in any opportunity that arises, but it must be of real help to others, not just you imagining that you are giving help. Learn to stand up to the pressures of life. Learn to face a hostile environment; do not always escape to a soft spot where you can enjoy yourself more. If you are a helper or a teacher, do not take credit for your power to make things happen satisfactorily. Work on adjusting your psychology all the time so that you can maintain a steady, even balance. Never allow yourself to be spoiled by anyone, including yourself. Do what you can by yourself. If you are rich, do not rely on financial strength to always hire somebody to do the things you should do yourself. If you are poor, do not be lazy and neglect details; accomplish all things that need to be done. Learn to be cooperative with reasonable people. Be a student of wise ones rather than be a leader or teacher of a group of fools. Make no excuse for what is your own fault. Never be argumentative in an attempt to justify your faults but admit them, compensate for them and strengthen them immediately.

A diamond character is to be nurtured among all gems. A truly virtuous character is the diamond of life.

3. Study Materials for the Diamond Level:
*Tao, the Subtle Universal Law (key book for
    spiritual learning)*
Internal Alchemy: The Natural Way to Immortality
Workbook for Spiritual Development
The Gentle Path of Spiritual Progress
Moonlight In the Dark Night
The Mystical Universal Mother
Esoteric Tao Teh Ching

Select the spiritual practices that best suit you and keep doing them.

If an exercise tape is chosen, Gentle Path T'ai Chi Movement is suggested to be learned as one of the study activities. A student can also select self-defense and confidence-building types of martial arts, or Chi Gong practices for general health or specific physical problems to fulfill the requirement of exercise which is very important.

The Crystal Level of the Integral Way of Life

1. The Goal: Is your mind your life support? Or, is your mind a traitor that always causes your kingdom of life to be troubled? What part of the mind is a good administrator of your life? What part of the mind is a troublemaker? Is the troublemaker internal pressure or is it external pressure? Is the trouble in your life other people's fault, your own fault or the fault of society? What is the solution and the remedy -- in the short run or the long run?

How do you take external pressure? How do you maintain your life on the right path? How do you become a reasonable being toward yourself and your surroundings? Is there a reward for your effort or not? What or who is the true teacher, guide or guardian who is always available to you? How do you attain help from your hidden partners, your developing spirits?

2. The Requirement: All the things you bring about in your life come from your mind. Most people think that the mind is the intellect, but the intellect brings troubles and burdens

to your life. The intellect is a function of the mind, it is not the whole mind. If people looked carefully, they would see that most of the time they do not determine how their life is going to be by their intellect. If people could choose their lives by the power of the intellectual mind, leaders would already have built a paradise for all people. Unfortunately, most people, including ambitious ones, do not even know how to make the distinction between the many functions of the mind which confuse or support each other. They do not know which compartments of the mind should be valued and which ones should be guarded against, listened to or ignored. Only through quiet spiritual cultivation can one learn to manage the different faculties of a complete mind.

Where is the balance of mind? What is clarity of mind? Intellectual study cannot help. Even a whole library of books and pictures will not help your life. What will help you is enlightenment. Enlightenment cannot be found by a faculty of mind. Enlightenment is close to spirit. A brightened, illumined mind functions when you start to meet trouble, particularly spiritual trouble. Typically, most people wait until trouble begins before they have the impetus to look to their mind for bright and sharp guidance. Enlightenment is not external help; it is internal growth. It is a spiritual breakthrough. Therefore, in this stage, you begin to work on enlightenment aside from other necessary practices and studies by facing the challenges and problems in your life. Enlightenment is not something that comes in 7 days, 7 years or even 70 years. At least, now you know how to start to cross the threshold between darkness and brightness of spiritual reality.

3. Study Materials for the Crystal Level:
Enlightenment: Mother of Spiritual Independence (Key Book)
Attaining Unlimited Life
The Way of Integral Life

Awaken to the Great Path[1]
Ascend the Spiritual Mountain
Essence of Universal Spirituality
Harmony - the Art of Life

Select the spiritual practices that fit you most and keep doing them.

An exercise tape should be chosen and learned as one of the study activities. Sky Journey is the recommended choice. A student can also select self-defense and confidence-building types of martial arts, or select Chi Gong practices for general health or specific physical problems to fulfill the requirement of exercise which is very important.

The Pearl Level of the Integral Way of Life
1. The Goal: What is the spiritual truth? To what truth can you conform your life? What is the way you make the life truth support you? How can you be the truth? Do you have spiritual confusion? What basic guidance and guidelines in your life do you now lean upon or feel you have solidly reached? Upright characteristics, not a rigid personality, can support your spiritual strength throughout hundreds of generations without making you feel ashamed by worldly suffering. What is your spiritual essence? Do you have one? How can you prove to yourself that you have one?

2. The Requirement: This is the Mystical Pearl. At this stage of your attainment, the Mystical Pearl is not intellectual achievement. It is a spiritual reality in which your mind is never stuck in enjoyment, trouble or any external pressure. A pearl can roll around with freedom, or it can stay still. It can be agitated but it does not fall apart. This signifies high spiritual growth. By the time you reach this stage, there should be no conflict within your own mind. There should be

---

[1]The *Uncharted Voyage Toward the Subtle Light* was divided to make two volumes, *Awaken to the Great Path* and *Ascend the Spiritual Mountain*. Either *The Uncharted Voyage Toward the Subtle Light* or the two new volumes may be studied to fulfill the requirement of this level.

no question of your being selfless or having self-interest because you will have transcended both. The study of books only becomes a part of cultivation. Your life and your service now take the place of books to be the refining process of your Mystical Pearl.

At this Level, selfless service is required. This can be considered as spiritual merit.

Description of Selfless Service

Traditionally, service was termed as spiritual merit or virtuous fulfillment. Spiritual merit can be divided into five types:

1. Spiritual sacred merit
2. Physical spiritual merit
3. Financial spiritual merit
4. Spiritual merit of service to specific individuals
5. Spiritual merit of service to society

1. Spiritual sacred merit.

This type of activity helps someone change their life attitudes from evil to virtuous, from trouble-making to considerate. Because evil is something which is expressed on a specific occasion, it is generally difficult to actually decide that someone is evil. Therefore, a spiritual student of sensitivity and knowledge tries to help people before they engage in evil (i.e., harmful) behavior and help people eliminate evil intentions. This can be done through subtle suggestion. Such a person sets a good example by their own actions. This person also explains the result of being evil.

Anyone who has a tendency to be harmful toward others or toward themselves might be helped by a moral or spiritual approach. A spiritual student can learn to exercise her or his subtle influence over others; likewise, he can learn to avoid negative influences and receive positive influences. This is the true way spiritual people can improve the world.

2. Physical spiritual merit.

Modern life lacks physical activity. In addition to seriously adopting some physical exercise programs into your daily life, also use your physical strength to clean and straighten where you live, which is also a good form of exercise.

3. Financial spiritual merit.
Be financially self-responsible. Choose to use money wisely and correctly. Use your financial strength to help and broaden spiritual activities. Before individual spiritual development, people are generally like the natural force of water or fire, which needs to be guided into good functions for society and the individual self.

4. Spiritual merit of service to specific individuals
Some people have special skills or achievements which can be exchanged for earning money or making a living. Such skills and achievement can also be applied to a moral purpose such as helping weak, old and/or needy individuals, or donating time to make a broad, spiritual service available to many people.

5. Spiritual merit of service to society
Spiritual merit is a service given without interfering, meddling or being aggressive in the affairs of others. Preferably, spiritual service can be given appropriately and correctly without draining oneself by external praise, admiration or pride.
Life takes many directions and offers different opportunities, but the best spiritual merit one can promote is to guide the world toward spiritual growth in the direction of peace, harmony, decency, happiness and enjoyment.
Very few people are born evil, bad or exceptionally good. Most people have troubles caused by the influences of social trends, fashion or real life experience. They just do not know how to select their position. The broad, open type of spiritual education that the ancient teaching of Tao (not the later folk religious Taoism) offers is practical in that it enables people to help themselves and others become wise individuals. People need to understand what is good and bad for them, the real significance of life, what is worthy and what is not worthy of pursuit. All clear, healthy minds can see that, but a healthy mind comes from a healthy social and cultural

environment. In the commercial world, the natural growth of personality is easily corrupted by all kinds of temptations as well as unnecessary competition and struggle. Therefore, it is easy to become lost, and even in old age a person may still not know what he or she lives for. A mature, common effort to help others can change our lives to be healthy, productive, useful and worthy of living. A community which offers such a useful service can be greatly valued.

3. Study Material for the Pearl Level:
Book of Changes and the Unchanging Truth (Key Book)
Footsteps of the Mystical Child
Guide to Inner Light
Internal Growth Through Tao
Story of Two Kingdoms
Power of Natural Healing

Continue to do the spiritual practices which fit you best.
An exercise tape should be chosen as one of the study activities. Infinite Expansion T'ai Chi Movement is a recommended choice. A student can also choose self-defense and confidence-building types of martial arts, or select Chi Gong practices for general health or specific physical problems to fulfill the requirement of exercise.

The Jade Level of the Integral Way of Life
1. The Goal: Are you a slave of life? Are you a slave to the world? Or are you a master of life? Have you achieved mastery of the life flow of society and universal nature? When you come to this level, your life essence has become the center of your life. It makes all other things you have or do not have, such as name, fortune, relationship, merit, etc., of secondary importance to this precious center. How do you know this center of life? It is not usually recognized because it is much more subtle than the faculties of the mind. How do you experience your center of life, the essence of your life? It is the fruit of spiritual cultivation. By your own achievement, you know that this center is what you are born with and what you live with, yet you have not developed it.

2. The Requirement: A valuable piece of jade represents that which is immaculate and flawless. In human life, most people experience disappointment, heartbreak or despair at some time. It is difficult to remain unaffected. However, spiritually, at this stage, we keep purifying ourselves. Keep yourself away from a position which rides an unclear line between the right and left, or using this situation to seek refuge from the hidden darkness. This is the spiritual goal of life.

Whatever life experience we have in the world, our soul is never defeated, although there can hardly be reason for arrogance in self achievement or any big contribution given to the world. At least spiritually, we not only keep whole and intact, we are spiritually rich people who have something to give to help others. We do what is right and what is beneficial to the situation we are in, without self credit. To lead this type of life is not too far from God. To live this type of life is to be a living God; it is not necessary to wear a white robe to show your spirituality. One can be wearing regular clothing while giving service and still attain the essence. To serve the world is to serve yourself.

Before you do anything, you need to judge whether it is right to do it or not. This means, to know the 'last judgement' before you engage in any behavior. You do not have to lie in a tomb for 1,000 years and wait for a postponed spiritual judgement in which it is decided whether you will ascend or descend. Even when we are in the process of doing or finishing something, we still have a chance to improve it, so we need to make a judgement about the righteousness and correctness of what we are doing. Putting the 'last judgement' in the very moment you are finishing a thing gives you an opportunity to make corrections. By correcting your possible deviation from the subtle law, you reach the level where there is no longer any question about whether you have a good or bad soul. You know that if you live with purity, you are a living angel. Spiritual accomplishment is your life. Your life is fragrant at any time, even long after your physical body stops living. Living a life of purity and service is a greater achievement than finding holy relics, which are the special spiritual gems found in the cremated ashes of a nun or monk.

So in this stage, the requirement is more hours of service or financial contribution (depending upon your situation) toward something meaningful and by your own wise choice.

3. Study materials for the Jade Level:
Eternal Light (Key Book)
Nurture Your Spirits
Quest of Soul
Taoist Inner View (Advanced Book)
Life and Teaching of Two Immortals: Volume I and Volume II
Mysticism: Empowering the Spirit Within
From Diversity to Unity
The Way, the Truth and the Light
Immortal Wisdom
By the Light of the North Star

Continue to do those spiritual practices that fit you most.
The exercise tapes become one of your study activities. Cosmic Tour Ba Gua Zahn is a recommended choice. A student can also select self-defense and confidence-building types of martial arts, or select Chi Gong practices for general heath or specific physical problems to fulfill the requirement of exercise which is very important.

List of Optional (not required) Study Materials for any Level:
Crane Style Chi Gong
The Tao of Nutrition
Chinese Vegetarian Delights
101 Vegetarian Delights
Chinese Herbology Made Easy
Ageless Counsel for Modern Life
Gentle Path T'ai Chi Chuan
Sky Journey T'ai Chi Chuan
Infinite Expansion T'ai Chi Chuan
Cosmic Tour T'ai Chi Chuan
T'ai Chi Chuan: An Appreciation
Chi Gong for Stress Release Audio Cassette
Chi Gong for Pain Management Audio Cassette
Tao Teh Ching Audio Cassettes
Invocations Audio Cassette

Chapter 2:
The Second Stage of Spiritual Achievement: Realization

The Five Phases of Integral Way of Life Realization

The focus of the Five Levels of Integral Way of Learning is on personal understanding, through studying the books and through learning and doing exercises. The focus of the Five Phases of Realization is different. The system of classification is the "Rose" Phase, the "Jasmine" Phase, the "Plum Blossom" Phase, the "Orchid" Phase and the "Lotus Flower" Phase of the Integral Truth of Life Realization or Service. After you complete this stage of spiritual achievement, that of virtuous fulfillment, you obtain the highest range of spiritual achievement, which is more invisible and less describable to the common eye. Thus, in the middle stage, you do your service, fulfill your virtue and refine yourself by living in the world and working with people. You use every occasion to externalize your learning. There are no certificates given for this achievement, but you may receive special instruction or teaching, as you have for all your fulfillments.

Service or virtuous fulfillment should be clearly understood. To raise children, whether of natural birth or adopted, is a type of virtue. Being a dutiful mother or father is a virtuous fulfillment. Taking care of one's parents or widowed elders has the same significance. A job which supports you and benefits people is also a virtuous fulfillment when done with devotion. Service or virtuous fulfillment should not only be narrowed down to public service.

The "Rose" Phase of Integral Truth of Life Realization or Service - Learning to take care of oneself, physically and mentally and not relying on the help of others unless it is necessary.

The "Jasmine" Phase of Integral Truth of Life Realization or Service - Learning to do service for people you are related to in what they cannot accomplish by themselves.

The "Plum Blossom" Phase of Integral Truth of Life Realization or Service - Learning to do service to those you may not be related to but who need help from someone.

The "Orchid" Phase of Integral Truth of Life Realization or Service - Learning to help all people spiritually by service or teaching.

The "Lotus Flower" Phase of Integral Truth of Life Realization or Service - Learning to draw happiness from the achievement of other people you have helped.

No certificates are given. This is a type of personal realization which does not need any recognition other than the student's awareness of his own progress - internal recognition. Because life is not rigid, no distinct time division is made between the phases or stages, but a student will have self knowledge when the understanding or awareness of each phase has been realized by himself or herself. This is a learning process that occurs over time.

Self-Evaluation
Only the individual student knows how much change and improvement has been made. Evaluation is based on what the person has achieved and its application in life. It is not based upon what can be put in a frame and hung on a wall.

How to Evaluate Your Own Improvement
For the purpose of self-improvement, each person can use the "star system" to examine oneself each day. A colorful star can represent good work done or improvements made. A black dot can be given for transgressions. This internal or personal practice can be kept in a diary. The system of using a diary is for internal communication with your mind and with high energy of judgement. In other words, it is to help you communicate with yourself. With self-cultivation alone, you do not know where you are. External, intellectual learning is not enough; internal learning is also necessary for the growth of the self. Because in a group of people each person exercises high conscience, you cannot escape other

people's spiritual vision for what you are, what you have done and how you have improved yourself. Good spiritual quality in a person needs no words. Such a person is appreciated, respected and enjoyed.

Use the reflection of yourself and other people to know what you need to keep working on and improving yourself. This honing or refinement process corresponds to the ancient metaphor of using tons of raw material to produce a tiny essence. Use this same metaphor for your own spiritual achievement and the true value of life.

Only people who live with their own true spirit understand other people. Only people who accept themselves accept other people. By constantly applying oneself one can spiritually reach the true self, which cannot be done by the marriage system, family system, school system, social system or church system.

Virtuous Fulfillment or Actualization
of What Was Learned in the Five Phases

This self-study program of spiritual attainment builds spiritual individuals. Teaching or doing service is the virtuous fulfillment of a student. It is not required that any student become a teacher or server in the College of Tao. The type of service or teaching a student does is not governed by specific regulations.

For a student who chooses a different way to complete personal virtuous fulfillment than working directly or indirectly for the College of Tao, and for those students who just live a correct, good life, the College is also interested in receiving your one-page yearly report. The report is to establish communication and keep us notified of your progress and mailing address. It is also to determine the basis to receive a letter of eligibility to attend special seminars on esoteric practices at the College of Tao.

In the tradition of truthful Integral Way of Life Realization, giving service by being a teacher does not establish any authority or social position. It is just one way of virtuous fulfillment, one part or section of your entire spiritual cultivation. There are also other ways to accomplish virtuous fulfillment besides teaching, such as helping the accomplishment of any valuable work or service.

Service does not always mean on a big scale in society. The spirit of service should be expressed in your everyday life. Whether on a large or small scale, always keep in mind the distinction between social service and social ambition. More spiritual value is derived from giving social spiritual service than from having social ambition.

General Guidelines Or Suggestions
to One Who is a Teacher or Wishes to be One

1. The correct attitudes of a sincere teacher have already been outlined by Lao Tzu. Teach without personal intention or ambition. Take no credit for whatever you have done for anyone, and retreat from what you have accomplished. Always return to your spiritual center, and keep your spiritual freedom by not grasping for things. Give service with an attitude of non-attachment. In giving service, freedom of spirit is most highly valued.

2. The two purposes of teaching, A) as a profession to earn a living and B) as a service to others, will each shape the teacher or person differently. The former, formal teaching, is done by a teacher who advertises classes. The latter adopts the knowledge that teaching is an experience that can be used in one's personal spiritual growth. For best spiritual benefit, teaching should not be used for material support.

It takes many years to build a good teacher. Teaching is a job; it does not automatically mean spiritual achievement. Yet, a spiritually achieved one can do periodic teaching over a number of years when the person has interest in doing so.

It is suggested that a spiritual student try to do teaching for a minimum of three years. If a person teaches between five to seven years, he or she will become a good teacher. If a person teaches over ten years, this person will be molded with a certain habit. That can potentially create a problem. There is no particular spiritual benefit to being molded as a teacher. However, it does not mean that no one should teach more than ten years. Rather, one should remain open, flexible and humble as long as one is teaching.

3. A teacher should not be ambitious to gather people that commit themselves to him or her. He or she teaches and serves the size of group which his or her spiritual energy can reach. In serving people, it is necessary to be careful that one's actions create no sacrifice to others. Teaching work is a matter of taking on difficulty, especially if you become too involved. However, if you are ready to make a commitment to serve others and take on some difficulty, it can surely be done as part of your virtuous fulfillment.

4. A spiritual teacher who uses spiritual teaching to gain everything he needs in life exchanges his spiritual quality for worldly needs. This is shallow and goes nowhere. Thus, just being a spiritual teacher does not guarantee real spiritual attainment. It can be pitiful if such a person lives in the world, uses his mouth and mind to serve people, but never receives the spiritual benefit of his own work.

Spiritual work and teaching is real service when it comes from those who do not use it as a social tool in life. I do encourage people to do social service just for their virtuous fulfillment. Virtuous fulfillment can remove the bad "karma" accumulated throughout many lives. On the plus side, it can build good "karma" for one's spiritual future.

However you look at it, true spiritual achievement comes from oneself. The truthful being of life is more spiritually grounded than the social being of a life. As you work with your society, keep this in mind and always watch what result it has on your spiritual being.

5. A) A formal teacher charges people for classes and so forth. This creates a situation of exchange through a fair charge or fee.

B) Informal teaching and pure spiritual service selects no particular object or particular person as its student. There is no charge; you are a pure giver. In learning the Integral Way of Life, informal teaching is highly esteemed. Yet, service through informal teaching cannot be given correctly by a person if he or she is unable to support himself financially. In the true spirit of life, informal teaching and informal

spiritual service is more highly esteemed than formal teaching, but both are important or necessary.

6. Informal teaching or service can be applied to any feasible
situation. It is suggested that a teacher not intentionally look
for situations, nor make decisions about the length of service
or what teaching will be given to whom. Allow it to happen
spontaneously. It is wisdom when a spiritual student uses
occasions of teaching or serving to refine oneself without
being limited by a particular structured situation that would
create negative feelings on either sides.

7. It is important that the relationship between teacher and
students be non-committal. The position of teacher creates
no power or authority. The position of teacher should not
exercise undue influence over anyone in practical matters.
Otherwise it would be a typical worldly game which produces
no spiritual benefit. A teacher should be sincere and committed to sharing the truth while the student is committed to
learning the truth!

8. There are two types of people. One type does not like to
give service. The other type likes to be socially recognized as
a teacher. Either way reflects the need for correction in being
able to balance one's personality.

9. Each teacher is responsible for his or her own behavior.
Immature behavior should be restrained. One's behavior
should be in concert with one's words - one must exemplify
the truth.

10. When teaching, always guide people to direct their faith,
trust or belief in the teachings, philosophies and practices
rather than try to make people believe in oneself for the sake
of ego building.

11. Some young teachers or leaders have the problem of an
unrefined ego that could limit the development of their good
work. Being overly egotistic often creates personality conflicts
with others, which reduces the overall benefits of the bigger

goal, because that person's choice of friends is limited. Only being objective and open will bring a world with cooperative, clear, harmonious atmosphere for all people.

12. If a teacher has a defect in virtue, it is correct to straighten himself first. If there is a misunderstanding between teacher and students, the teacher needs to examine the matter and do what is necessary in the teaching and service.

13. To students and teachers who encounter the difficulties of others and discover the difficulties of themselves, the College motto given by Master Ni from his father is "Life and various work, to a spiritual student or a teacher, is spiritual cultivation like no other." It means that a student of the Integral Way as a natural life science regards the experiencing of life difficulties in various areas as something positive to be worked out. That is the most important aspect of spiritual cultivation. To fulfill a job or a duty is to do spiritual cultivation. To be somebody's husband or wife is a spiritual cultivation. To be somebody's father or daughter is a spiritual cultivation. Even being someone's boyfriend or girlfriend is also a spiritual cultivation. In all other situations, just use the external situation and position to discover and refine your inner self. This provides an opportunity to extend your spiritual service with direct value. Do not make anyone sacrifice for you and do not negatively cause suffering for others by making it necessary for them to live an ineffective life. If you do, then there is no real spiritual cultivation existing in your life, because there is no balance.

14. The purity and unity of individual spiritual quality will be lessened if one continually exposes oneself as the center of a small or big group of people. It is always wise to walk away at the correct time and circumstance from such a situation. Spiritually, it is sufficient to avail oneself in some position, imposing nothing on others and thus bringing no conflict in one's own further spiritual development.

There is wisdom in this tradition: do not stay in the crowd too long. Do not stay in a competitive position too long. In either situation, a crisis will eventually arise.

How to Teach for the College of Tao
How to Accomplish Your Virtuous Fulfillment
by Helping the College of Tao

Please refer to Appendix A for specific information.

Service is a Step on the Path

True spiritual achievement must come from one's own deep pursuit. Group activity alone cannot reach it. True spiritual achievement is not derived from being a teacher, but this kind of social spiritual service is one way of virtuous fulfillment. Teaching is more discipline than spiritual achievement. However, too much social activity will pull one away from the center of life, placing one's spiritual focus on the external struggle of trying to maintain balance rather than on true, high spiritual achievement. Social spiritual service makes a person spiritually selfless, so it is worthwhile to take a number of years to be with and to work for people.

If a student does not learn any really deep, truthful practice, then at least one's spiritual service to others will make one's spirit light and not as heavy as those whose life is spent amassing excessive fame, reputation, money, physical indulgence, pride, vanity, glory, etc. Although these things can be the by-products of a virtuous life. Some achieved ones dedicate their lives to benefit those people who have lightened their souls through service.

The one who masters a practice can assure the success of spiritual cultivation through virtuous fulfillment such as giving selfless spiritual service. Beginners and most students will find it best to work with people and frequently withdraw to find the balance between outward and inward spiritual interplay. This is a better way to reach potential spiritual attainment than becoming wholly socially involved. It is easy to lose oneself in the masses of the world and in society. Those who live in the world with society and at the same time have a deep spiritual life get more out of life.

Chapter 3:
The Third Stage of Spiritual Achievement:
Ascension or Sublimation

The Guideline for the Realization of Internal Alchemy

At the highest stage of spiritual achievement, the central focus is spiritual integration of oneself. It is the spiritual sublimation of oneself or one's own ascension. It does not mean that you die. When you enter this stage, there is a distinct line drawn between your previous life and the new one. Before, your life was being lived for death, or for the end result of death. In this stage, you live for the eternalness of life. You ascend from general conflict and worldly competition and not only find your spiritual unity within and without, but you also find truthful proof of a reality of life that is very different than what most people know. With your new spiritual reality, you can communicate with the external and internal spiritual existence. Your definition of individuality - habitual life attitudes - will diminish and be replaced by a new reality, happily so. This all happens even before you give up your physical being. You work toward ascension from the general conception of life. Finally you reach the goal of making ascension happen truthfully in your lifetime and are not waiting for something to happen after death.

The student who has reached this level of study and service may attend special seminars given by the College on esoteric subjects.

The Realization of Internal Alchemy

This is optional by a student's choice after finishing the above Five Levels and Five Phases. You may wish to obtain special high instruction for this practice.

If you choose to learn and practice internal alchemy, the traditional attainment is given as follows:

1. Transform sexual fluid to be vaporized and rise to the higher area of the body.

2. Channel the chi (vaporized energy) in orbit circulation.

3. Crystalize the chi to be particles of semi-spiritual energy. (Attain strong psychic, subtle communication power, healing power).

4. Converge the semi-spirit to be spirit, psychic or intuitive.

5. Strengthen the spirit to be light - silver and gold light. Bear the fruit of spiritual cultivation, which is to conceive the yang spirit or spiritual baby.

6. Form the light to be a subtle body like yourself.

7. Achieve the freedom to form and unform the subtle body.

8. Unite individual spiritual attainment with the subtle origin and attain immortality.

Addendum:
More Guidelines for Students
Who Use the Self-Study Program

It is important spiritual knowledge for all students of the College of Tao that a short invocation is more effective than a long prayer. Constant repetition of the same prayer is more effective than inconsistent prayer for different things. Prayer in concentration, calmness and quietude is more effective than prayer done with strong emotion and struggle.

A less personal prayer will establish a higher personal spiritual stature than prayers which are done out of selfishness. If a response is received for the appropriate thing in life, it mean that an individual's personal spiritual energy is growing. A person should not pray for anything negative, because negative wishes means that a person is too partial or petty minded. It means that the person is being careless rather than selective in shaping one's spiritual reality. Nonverbal prayer through one's life and behavior is stronger and more useful than any spoken words.

All students of the College of Tao need to pray daily. In the morning, and the evening they pray quietly by the mind or gentle voice:

Let there be peace on earth.
May freedom triumph.
May people of insufficient means
*   attain improvement.*
May the world remove all artificial disasters.
May people who enjoy freedom use their opportunity
*   to achieve themselves spiritually.*
May the world's people awaken to love their home,
*   the Earth, and not allow industrial pollution*
*   to become a common disaster.*

Each student can also pray:

Let me not lose a balanced mind
*   in viewing other people.*
Let me be the strength that brings about
*   my own healthy being and*

helps bring about a healthy world.
Let my internal spiritual growth be above my interest
in material or emotional expansion.
Let my lifetime of self-cultivation bring me
to achieve myself so that I need no more
experiences of self-created misery.
Let us not forget, as we work toward
our learning and realization,
that we are not working for ourselves alone,
but also for all others.

The Self-Study Program and Correspondence Course is a supplement to the *Golden Message* from Master Ni.

APPENDIX A

To accomplish your virtuous fulfillment, if you choose to be a teacher of arts and sciences of the Integral Way of Life in this tradition, the following guidelines will apply to you.

The College wishes to directly serve individuals and small private groups. For those wishing to use Master Ni's books for public teaching or other use, permission is required from the College of Tao.

1. All the guidelines mentioned above for general teachers apply to you.

2. Students who wish to teach specific material or practices from Master Ni's books or who wish to teach gentle movement must apply for authorization. There will be a fee for a certificate of authorization. Send a letter stating your interest to the College of Tao with your background, skills and knowledge. You will be contacted for an interview and a skills demonstration. Be sure you are adept at performing the movements and teaching, or that you are proficient with the material in the book(s) and are able to teach it. Do not waste your time and trip without thorough preparation.

Teaching categories which need specific certification from the College are as follows: Teacher of Eight Treasures, Dao-In, Trinity T'ai Chi, Gentle Path, Sky Journey, Infinite

Expansion T'ai Chi Chuan, Cosmic Tour Ba Gua, Chi Gong, meditation and other specific spiritual practices.

3. Those who wish to teach Master Ni's written material must send a separate letter of intent to obtain written authorization. If you wish to teach, there are other requirements such as an interview or teaching demonstration by the College.

4. The authorization to teach Master Ni's written materials will be valid for three years. At the expiration date, a teacher must send the Authorization back to the College of Tao with a one page written report.

Thus, all previously ordained ministers, mentors and assigned teachers are also asked to do the same with their letter or certificate.

The purpose of the three-year reports is for the teacher to extend the intent to continue the spiritual relationship with the Union of Tao and Man. After the renewal has been granted, the College will imprint the certificate or letter with another traditional Chop (red Chinese calligraphy imprint) and date it. These chops are of traditional spiritual value.

The three-year reports provide an opportunity for the individual teacher to reflect on their progress and deficiencies and to express their desire to continue working with the College. We will also keep your name on our mailing list. Thus, although all teachers are independent, the communication expresses the relationship between the teacher and the College.

This requirement also applies to the teachers certified to teach physical movement, although as time progresses, they will generally become more skillful. The movement teachers still need to give a three year report and receive a dated chop.

5. The Shrine of the Eternal Breath of Tao has produced eight videotapes, five with companion books, on gentle movement. Some people have learned these movement techniques from the videotapes. Those who have learned from the tapes or from teachers of various centers of this tradition and wish to attain authorization to teach movement should apply to the College of Tao. For the purpose of having

a unified standard for those who wish to teach skills of movement, a special teachers' seminar should be attended and a written teacher's certificate must be obtained from the College. Make sure that you are ready or have been approved by the local teacher if you have one. Otherwise, avoid wasting your time and trip. There will be a standard charge for the certificate. All authorization to teach given by the College or Master Ni must be in written form.

6. Giving service by being a teacher is one way of virtuous fulfillment. Thus, a teacher must be self-reliant. This means he or she needs to have a regular job or business, or enough personal financial strength for self-support. Although there are potential pitfalls that a teacher of many years' experience may encounter, the Integral Truth never fails to encourage a virtuous and developed individual to continue to render service for any length of time while the sun still moves.

7. A teacher may charge people who attend the formal classes, but the charge must be fair. Teachers may not ask their students to tithe. If they do so, the money is to be used strictly to serve the spiritual purpose. People can also make special donations for a clear purpose.

8. A teacher who wishes to earn one's living through teaching can learn some exercises to teach like the Eight Treasures and at least one other kind of movement or some meditation skill. If possible, a teacher can also learn or develop some counseling skills. This school does not discourage useful teaching as a means of life support.

9. Thus far, some teachers partially or totally adopt the teaching of Natural Life Science (the Integral Way). The College will give support, and asks nothing from anyone. The College is dedicated to offering social service. All people who utilize Master Ni's material to help themselves or others are equally accepted by the College. The College itself is non-profit. Currently, it is supported by the Ni family.

10. There are no special relationships between the College and any of the teachers. The teachers' good spirit is offered selflessly to serve the world by doing this teaching. The only standard established to rule out who should or should not teach is based on an individual's virtuous intention to help others, deep understanding and realization of the materials from this tradition and a sincere attitude toward one's personal spiritual development. As long as the teacher does nothing against the tenets of the Integral Way they can continue to be recognized or supported by the College.

11. In general, all teachers need to learn meditation techniques at different levels. We hope teachers who have achieved the depth of self-cultivation have personal spiritual achievement such as sexual energy sublimation will also accomplish other useful practices to help the world without becoming a type of religious teacher.

12. A teacher must always remember not to make the tradition support him or her but to be a good representative of the pure reputation of the tradition. The teaching of the Integral Way is pure and truthful. It is not a rigid religious tradition that creates obligations and corresponding privileges. Master Ni does not recommend this kind of operation.

13. A teacher must first make sure that what he or she has learned from this spiritual source serves him or her well. After being sure that any practices and teachings are useful and the teacher has been truly helped by the practices or learning, then it is appropriate to teach others. Otherwise, the practices or teachings should not be recommended or taught to other people.
   When a teacher does recommend those things to other people, never impose one's beliefs or practices but let people take them as a suggestion. One suitable way of teaching is to suggest the practice and give students an opportunity to try it without making any kind of commitment.

14. All teaching material produced by Master Ni needs to be carefully studied by a student as he or she goes through

different stages of development. Some students will work harder than others to understand and study Master Ni's books. However, if a person has not purified oneself from mental and spiritual confusion and contamination, there is bound to be confusion, misapplication of the teachings and complication. Therefore, life needs constant purification every day you are in the world. Being a living God is much more difficult than being a dead role model. A role model is a dead standard; it is a life that has been accomplished. A living God needs to constantly have spiritual discipline, purification, refinement, emotional attunement and physical strengthening in order to accomplish one's spiritual journey in life.

15.   Once appointed by Master Ni as certified mentors, teachers can appoint assistant teachers to help them teach exercise.

16.   It is preferred that the teachers who use Master Ni's material also have good personal living skills. In order to assure that teachers have a basic understanding of healthy living and achievement in the learning of one or several movements, they must not only obtain authorization to teach movement, but also obtain a certificate for having completed the self-study course of Master Ni's books.

17.   Some teachers who have been personally inspired by Master Ni or who have in the past taken classes from Master Ni are now using his material to establish their teaching. In reality, each teacher presents oneself and organizes one's teaching material by adopting the teaching of the Integral Way. Therefore, whatever these teachers choose to teach in association with Master Ni's material shall present themselves instead of representing this tradition.

18.   The true spirit of an ancient achieved one is different from social doctrines and later religions. It encourages the next generation to do better than the previous, the student to do better than the teacher and allows all other people to do better than oneself. One only needs to strengthen oneself. It means when you adopt other people's teaching, you allow

people's teaching to be what it is. Never twist or apply it only to support the insufficiencies of your personality.

Master Ni accepts and gives support to people who utilize his material in their teaching with his permission. However, he will feel misused if some people apply his teaching, not for their own truthful growth to really surpass themselves but to support their ego, stubbornness, greed or any other weak and dark personality trait.

19. The College welcomes teachers who share the same basic attitude toward not making people one's personal, private students, but students of the Integral Way. Master Ni considers his teaching appropriate to be used at one stage as a help for their further growth.

20. Incorrect use of Master Ni's materials include making an improper combination with materials from other religions. The College of Tao and/or Master Ni may determine whether use of certain materials is correct or incorrect. The College and Master Ni reserve the right to withdraw previous permission granted to teachers and centers to avoid the unintended effect of his work.

21. A teacher cannot franchise Master Ni's teaching to someone else. A teacher assists other individuals with the same good intention to serve others. The principle is that Master Ni does not charge anyone with financial or any other commitment for the use of his materials.

22. Remember, teaching is a service, a virtuous fulfillment, not an occupation in this tradition. People have different stages of growth. If you make spiritual service or teaching a profession or occupation it will have a negative effect on you by causing you to become too externalized. You will lose your spiritual essence by becoming attached to a worldly position or work.

Guidelines for Setting up a Center
for Learning the Integral Way

Some teachers may want to set up a center and use Master Ni's books as a teaching service with particular skills involved such as T'ai Chi Chuan, martial arts, psychotherapy or a type of spiritual service in teaching activities. This type of center needs permission from the College or from Master Ni; contact Maoshing Ni. The broad and open approach is also acceptable to the College, but the College prefers that only one single pure spiritual teaching be used because an improper mixture would cause confusion that would hinder students' healthy spiritual growth.

1. The teaching function and purpose of the College and of the centers are different. The centers' goal is to promote people's interest in learning spiritual information, or to learn exercises and practices to help their lives. The College intends to help short or long term study and to better prepare people for teaching service or for real spiritual achievement. The centers and the College can work together to assist each other with different functions.

2. If a teacher organizes a teaching center, the financial strength to support a center comes from the teacher. The expenses of maintaining a center comes from the teacher's income from teaching and service activities. If any support comes from the students, they must have the truthful understanding and sincerity to make the donation as part of their financial service to others. It becomes a part of their own virtuous fulfillment. Such financial virtuous fulfillment can be considered a service or mutual service between the teacher and students. This type of healthy social activity is one way of love. However, the teacher needs to maintain his or her discipline, become financially independent and self-reliant and not use the financial contributions for his or her life support.

3. If you are interested in setting up a center, please contact Frank Gibson, The Center for Taoist Arts, PO Box 1389, Alpharetta, GA 30239-1389.

Certificate of Completion Program for Individual Skills

College of Tao
Director: Maoshing Ni, Ph.D.

Purpose: to provide students with a complete program of in-depth and thorough learning in various fields of Natural Life Science.   Completion of each program will enable each participant to help raise his or her quality of life and to be of service to others.

Description: Each program will consist of primarily two learning modules - correspondence and seminars. Students are required to complete the correspondence portion within a set time and attend seminars.

Programs: Below is a partial list of subjects/fields available or being prepared for the Certificate Program. Please write for information and availability of each subject/field.

Nutrition of Natural Life Science
Therapeutic Cooking
Massage and Tui-Na
Chinese Herbology
Cosmology (life chart reading based on natural life science)
Internal Arts of Gentle Movement (from the tradition of the School of Internal Harmony):
    Chi Gong
    Eight Treasures
    Individual T'ai Chi forms
    Ba Gua
    Dao In
    Sword forms
    others
Geomancy
Physiognomy
Meditation and Spiritual Practices of the Integral Way
Integral Education
Personal Counseling
Business and lifestyle management of the Integral Way

Traditional Chinese Medicine: Acupuncture and Herbology (approved Masters Degree through Yo San University)

Tuition: Varies from program to program depending on length and number of seminars required.

Please write: College of Tao
                       Attention: Certificate Program
                       1314 Second Street, Suite A
                       Santa Monica, CA 90401

                          *   *   *

     The College of Tao was established in 1979 and approved by the State of California as a religious school. The College grants degrees like any other religious school in the United States. Because the government does not have any experience with spiritual traditions other than religions, the Union of Tao and Man conforms to the regulations of being organized as a church. It can grant a degree similar to Doctor of Divinity, but Doctor of Natural Life Science will be given as an acknowledgement of achievement from the College only to qualified teachers who have mastered the subject.

Part VII

Being a Student and a Teacher

Spiritually achieved people are trained to share their achievement with the world. The ancient achieved ones offered their good service in various ways. Lao Tzu himself told us that spiritual wealth is subject to the law that "You receive as much as you give," and, "When you give more, you have more." This implies that the nature of spiritual wealth is inexhaustible.

Spiritual wealth is built by no private intention, manipulation or dominance. Lao Tzu openly said that you earn worldwide friendship by doing nothing. By this, he means that it is not through any conquering measure such as war or espionage that ambitions or desires are realized. Great spiritual accomplishment happens through pure spiritual response.

In general, there are three types of spiritual students or people who aspire to spiritual achievement, which is both internal and external. The first type has a reclusive or introverted personality and wishes to find a reason or excuse to withdraw from the world. What this type of student achieves is a rationalization for escaping from the world, nothing more.

The second type of student is a dependant personality. This type depends upon psychological support from skillfully worded teachings and is more agreeable to have around when he or she knows nothing about spirituality. This type of student is generally more agreeable than the other two, because they retain the potential to grow and to achieve if they have the right destination. The correct destination for all spiritual students is first to achieve spiritual health and balanced internal strength. After growing stronger, one's healthy spiritual strength can help other people. Spiritual health can wither if you do not make correct use of it through unselfish application.

The third type of student has an aggressive personality and uses spiritual learning as an excuse for aggression. If they could be achieved, what they achieve is a rationalization for their aggressive personality. This is the same as the first type of student who also fools himself by twisting a good, broad spiritual teaching to rationalize his personality.

The first type of withdrawn personality usually causes no big harm to the world, but sometimes causes trouble by denying personal responsibility. If the third type of aggressive personality chooses spiritual teaching or social leadership as a life activity, harm will come from his or her activities.

The way for a student or teacher to avoid the trap of personality described by the first withdrawn type and the third aggressive type is to learn and adapt the following information:

Most people's spirit is very unstable. What stabilizes people's spiritual energy is their physical form. Once you are born and materialized within a physical body, conflict between the spirit and the body will happen when you move toward growth without spiritual cultivation. So-called spiritual discipline is not discipline given to your life spirit, but is given to your intellectual, physical and emotional levels of being. You do not need to apply discipline to what you do not do, but to what you do. This means that you do not need to apply discipline to the subtle substance of your life, but to your activities. Apply discipline to excessive physical desires and excessive ambition of the mind.

Ancient spiritually achieved ones called the subtle substance or pure spiritual energy "pre-Heaven." They called the body "post-Heaven." Each person's life is the union of pre-Heaven (spirit) and post-Heaven (body). Pre-Heaven (spirit) cannot be known or function by itself unless it is combined with the post-Heaven (body). In worldly life, pre-Heaven relies on post-Heaven, at least on the physical plane of life.

Pre-Heaven is God and post-Heaven is the physical world. The two rely upon each other for existence, but reliance upon the physical is not the purpose or function of pre-Heaven or God. The function of the pre-Heaven part of your existence is to harmonize with the physical. In order to help an individual reach harmony or unity between these two, there is spiritual cultivation. Spiritual cultivation finds the point that prevents too many worldly concerns from burdening the spirit, and prevents an ascetic type of life which promotes spirituality through neglecting or damaging the physical body by self-punishing discipline.

This discussion contains many dualistic ideas. The ancient achieved ones did not have as many words or literary works as I have presented to you. My work presents a picture to help your depth of vision. It is necessary to guide you through different planes in order for you to attain such vision. A picture of a carrot is printed on a piece of paper. The typical observer will only see the image of the carrot and will not see the blank paper upon which the image of the carrot has been imposed. This is a metaphor that expresses the existence of spiritual truth.

I hope that this short instruction helps you see how to have a balanced, not extreme, personality. This is what I have been discussing in many of my books, using different approaches. Each individual has a world for himself or herself to handle. If you can manage yourself well and stay peaceful and unified without allowing extremes of either the spiritual or physical side to be expressed, you are on the way to eternal life. To put it another way, if you remain balanced, you attain spiritual truth.

It is the dualistic reality of the earth plane which establishes some individuals as authorities, teachers, leaders, popes, bishops, abbots, patriarchs, etc. Titles, however, have no spiritual value but are either for recognition of an individual's achievement by the unachieved or for egotistical purposes. Real spiritual influence can be offered to people simply by concentrating in one's own spiritual cultivation. If you are a teacher, your good spiritual influence can help your students more by maintaining your own self-cultivation. It is a result of your internal spiritual achievement externalized by your own cultivation. All external things, including those used as teaching tools, are untruthful. Objects, such as religious statues, in and of themselves have no spiritual value; their true value is to attract the spiritual energy response from your mind. In other words, nothing external can make you more spiritual.

Spiritual balance comes from learning to manage yourself and your life with harmony and unity. You cannot require other people to have the same achievement. No person can require another person to be spiritually balanced, because it is an individual attainment. Yet, we can help other people learn spiritual cultivation to manage their lives and reach their own internal unity and harmony.

Jesus has been considered a perfect model of divine morality. He himself experienced the two sides of life: God and Satan. While he was alive, he found the correct way to unite both his spiritual and physical lives. He was a good example for his disciples. However, one person, even a godly or balanced person, cannot have power over all other people; thus, he was betrayed by one of his disciples. By this, it may appear that I am telling young teachers not to adopt students, because some students can be harmful. Based on this fact, refrain from physical contact, especially deep involvement such as money, power and sex. Once you reach your own personal essence, it is unspiritual to use it for recognition or social expansion. It is spiritual to be natural about what happens correctly in your life. Do not ask or require that certain things happen in your surroundings, but concentrate upon keeping your energy from flowing over the rim.

A young teacher who is recognized by the masses will no doubt encounter money, power and beautiful men and women surrounding him. When this temptation comes, oftentimes also comes corruption and failure, and the original spiritual cultivation is destroyed. This is sometimes called the power of Satan, or the "other side of life." It is wise to learn clearly about both sides of life before you become a teacher, preacher or evangelist and are always in the public eye. In this way, problems can be circumvented.

In my type of work, informal teaching is more important than formal teaching. In this way, you improve your personal life, such as family and social life. I also encourage my friends and students to become mentors or teachers and point out the independent responsibility of all those who become teachers when they teach in public.

There are friends who enjoy my teaching and organized study groups and adopt my work as their spiritual direction. I make all those teachers self-responsible for a number of reasons. First, they need to adapt to their own working and

living situation. Second, it is not necessary for their achievement and practical implementation to be the same as mine.
Third, each group should have their own agreed discipline; if
there are no suitable rules, disciplines and necessary rites,
the group can hardly be kept healthy. Fourth, in leadership,
each person has one's own stage of growth. With exposure to
different types of attraction and temptation, all possible
difficulties could happen to the teacher. Those situations
become opportunities for personal victory or chance for
personal difficulties.

Mistakes happen even to a righteous person. This is why
the ancient virtuous people cultivated themselves, but the one
who serves the public with correct teaching and conduct is
greater in virtuous fulfillment if he or she knows to hold onto
to the correct purpose, not to personal achievement. Thus, as
a teacher, I allow all people room to grow. The sense of
personal responsibility will become strong and firm among
everyone. One teacher offered a good intellectual service to
others, but mixed it with personal sexual practice, which
caused damage to his good contribution to people's minds.
After attaining some popularity, another teacher discovered
how to gather money and also began to lose spiritual discipline in sexual matters. I have nurtured teaching materials
and offer them to be used, but they are misused if such
things occur. We must use these examples as a warning to
keep our focus upon our spiritual cultivation and upon
offering help to those around us in their lives and spiritual
understanding. It is not wise to have multiple sexual relationships; it complicates one's life unnecessarily. If you are
a spiritual teacher, it is recommended that you maintain your
self discipline in order to avoid destroying the good work you
have accomplished. Yielding to temptation is not wise, even
though it is easily done. Avoid whatever society does not
accept because it will damage your work.

Too much organization, too much management or
reversely, not enough organization or management, all cause
problems. A helpful motto for my students who wish to
become a teacher or leader is this: Make your teaching the
unity of self-discipline and self-cultivation. Add nothing to
this. This is wisdom and knowledge. The success and

happiness which can be enjoyed for a long time is only obtained through unselfish ends and through a balanced way in all aspects of life.

I agree that spiritual teachers be supported by students at the level the students can afford. If you can, work to support your own life and make your teaching work an offering to society; this is my personal choice. However, any donation received from people should be used for the spiritual purpose of helping people.

Instruction from Our Father
Ni, Hua-Ching

A human being born into the world is the child of the universe. In the universe, there are two kinds of energy, yin and yang. These great natural energies take the shape of man and woman to bring your precious life with all of its possible beautiful fulfillment into the world. You are the son or daughter of Heaven and Earth. What else would you like to become? This opportunity of life is presented to you. The meaning of your life depends on whether you live fully, completely, effectively and enjoyably.

Yet some people, maybe you, are confused and lost in the colorful dust of cultural worldly creations. You would like to work hard to achieve or become something and earn your living. However, if you believe that what you have achieved or become is who you are, you have put something over your natural being. You have covered your true being, as in applying cosmetics.

People are abused by others who accept the general conception of the cultural establishment, or they abuse their own lives by their own ignorance.

In truth, religions are the way you choose to arrange your spiritual life. Your good choice depends upon your own spiritual development.

There is a spiritual education called the Integral Way. It tells you that you are an angel. I think angels are the most beautiful thing in the entire universe. What else would you like to become? Some people prefer to gain something from words out of the mouths of priests. Others wish to receive blessings from the hardship of practicing rituals. The greatest thing you can gain is the wholeness of your spiritual nature. Church will not save your spiritual nature.

There are all kinds of establishments that want to rob your true angel nature and replace it with hardness and force. If you follow such things, you lose sight of the preciousness of natural life. The truth of natural life can only be told from one angel to another angel. This is why I am telling it to you, because I know you are an angel, but you have just forgotten. Others do not accept that; they are too lost and cause trouble for others and themselves. For millions of years, achieved ones have been telling the truth to the people who are lost. These lost people are so full of the world's poison that they cannot see the truth.

Mao and Dao have done well in giving us the chapter on the teaching of the Integral Way. I am glad they know that such things cannot be kept to oneself.

It is the tension of life that causes one's conscience to become contorted. In the same way, people become selfish and evil. If you give up your tension and learn to relax as you fulfill your daily work, you can recover the preciousness and sacredness of your natural life being. You know, you have come here to Earth to enjoy life, not to suffer. Please understand that the word "enjoy" does not mean self-indulgence in all kinds of mixed enjoyment, or sipping the poisonous tonic of life. "Enjoy" means to have a safe, secure, contented, peaceful and quiet life.

As a healer, I offer my spare time to teach and write with the wish to guide you back to your natural angel life. That is the intention and purpose of this book, all my work, and all the sincere and correct teachers of the Integral Way. If you would like to realize paradise in your personal life, in the relationships with your friends and with all people, it is worth your while to spend some time to see what you can learn from reading my books.

Once a heavenly angel visited the human world. Eventually, by imitating the surrounding animals, the angel absorbed destructive habits and forgot who he was. However, his heavenly friends became anxious; they wished to find the lost angel and return him to their heavenly paradise. Another angel was sent down with the mission of finding the lost one, but the lost one could not be found. So, a map was left.

The map of how to return to this heavenly paradise has finally come into your hand. By following this map, it is possible to reach the heavenly paradise while you are living in the world. However, the task is yours. Nobody can lift an angel back to Heaven; an angel needs to lift itself.

The only correct way is to find the Integral Truth in your life. That can help you in this important restoration. Spiritual self-cultivation is no other than an effective and reasonable way to arrange your spiritual, mental and physical life. This teaching of the Integral Way seems only to make itself clear to the people who are ready, because it is spiritual development itself. Nevertheless, to call some people ready and other people not ready is somewhat inaccurate. People are in varying stages of readiness. Someone who might not appear ready may be on the verge of a breakthrough that could bring about the change. Others have a little more to learn. Therefore, no matter how ready or unready you feel, keep learning, keep trying.

On the journey of life, universal nature shaped human people, for has three million years. Many of our human ancestors were truly achieved. They are ahead of us on the way of spiritual evolution. They are ready to help your beautiful soul and to enjoy the highest spiritual paradise together with you.

The Integral Way is the remedy for human mistakes caused by the religious domination of society which created darkness for all people, and for the materialism exalted by the communist movement which has brought about no less darkness and calamity than religious dominance. The shortcoming of narrow religions and of new socio-political movements is the erroneous expression of unhealthy ideology produced by unhealthy, prejudicial minds. Religious idealism, socio-political movements, materialism and technological creations are all examples of irresponsible expansion. Any partial, extreme extension of science, technology or materialism brings about damage to individuals and society.

In a natural, healthy society, people have the freedom to choose their religious practice and to be open to higher spiritual education. At the same time, people need not create religions to evade the material obligations of their own lives.

Whether used by a society or an individual, the Integral Way recognizes the completeness of life and the need for exploration and development in different directions without losing the center of good, healthy, balanced people and societies. The Integral Way can also be considered the fruit of all human experience. Wise individuals and leaders of society benefit by consulting the history of the human world.

Integralism is the best representation of the naturalness and genuineness of human life. It expresses the natural health and completeness of human society, the earth's environment and universal nature itself.

People who attain maturity and wisdom do not exalt the extreme of any one direction. From this point, the value of the Integral Way by itself is presented for your scrutiny before you accept it as a philosophy and way of life.

About Hua-Ching Ni

Hua-Ching Ni is fully acknowledged and empowered by his own spiritual attainment rather than by external authority. He is a teacher of natural spiritual truth and a natural person. He is heir to the wisdom transmitted through an unbroken succession of numberless generations of true masters dating back to the time before written history. As a young boy, he was educated by his family in the foundation of the natural spiritual truth. Later, he learned spiritual arts from various achieved teachers, some of whom have a long traditional background, and fully achieved all aspects of ancient science and metaphysics.

In addition, 38 generations of the Ni family worked as farmers, natural healers and scholars. Master Ni has continued in America with clinics and the establishment of Yo San University of Traditional Chinese Medicine. Master Ni worked as a traditional Chinese doctor and taught spiritual learning on the side as a service to people. He taught first in Taiwan for 27 years by offering many publications in Chinese and then in the United States and other Western countries since 1976. To date, he has published about thirty books in English, made five videotapes of gentle movement and has written some natural spiritual songs sung by an American singer.

Hua-Ching Ni lived in the mountains at different stages. When possible, he stays part-time in seclusion in the mountains and part-time in the city doing work of a different nature. He believes this is better for his nervous system than staying in only one type of environment.

The books that he has written in Chinese include two books about Chinese medicine, five books about spiritual self-cultivation and four books about the Chinese internal school of martial arts. These were published in Taiwan. He has also written two unpublished books on ancient spiritual subjects related with natural health and spiritual development.

The other unpublished books were written by brush in Chinese calligraphy during the years he attained a certain degree of achievement in his personal spiritual cultivation. He said, "Those books were written when my spiritual energy was rising to my head to answer the deep questions in my mind. In spiritual self-cultivation, only by nurturing your own internal spirit can communication exist between the internal and external gods. This can be proven by your personal spiritual stature. For example, after nurturing your internal spirit, through your thoughts you contact many subjects which you could not reach in ordinary daily life. Such spiritual inspiration comes to help when you need it. Writings done in good concentration are almost like meditation and are one fruit of your cultivation. This type of writing is how internal and external spiritual communication can be realized. For the purpose of self-instruction, writing is one important practice of the Jing Ming School or the School of Pure Light. It was beneficial to me as I grew spiritually. I began to write when I was a teenager and my spiritual self-awareness had begun to grow."

In his books published in Taiwan, Hua-Ching Ni did not give the details of his spiritual background. It was ancient spiritual custom that all writers, such as Lao Tzu and Chuang Tzu, avoided describing their personal lives. Lao Tzu and Chuang Tzu were not even their names. However, Master Ni conforms with the modern system of biographies and copyrights to meet the needs of the new society.

Hua-Ching Ni's teaching differs from what is generally called Taoism, conventional religious Taoism or the narrow concept of lineage or religious mixture of folk Taoism. His teaching is non-conventional and differs from the teaching of any other teachers. He teaches spiritual self-sufficiency rather than spiritual dependence.

Master Ni shares his own achievement as the teaching of rejuvenated original spiritual truth, which has its origins in the prehistoric stages of human life. His teaching is the Integral Way or Integral Truth. It is based on the Three Scriptures of ancient spiritual mysticism: Lao Tzu's *Tao Teh Ching, The Teachings of Chuang Tzu* and *The Book of Changes.* He has translated and elucidated these three classics into versions which carry the accuracy of the valuable ancient message. His other books are materials for different stages of learning the truth. He has also absorbed all the truthful high spiritual achievements from various schools to assist the illustration of spiritual truth with his own achieved insight on each different level of teaching.

The ancient spiritual writing contained in the Three Scriptures of ancient spiritual mysticism and all spiritual books of many schools were very difficult to understand, even for Chinese scholars. Thus, the true ancient spiritual teaching from the oriental region is not known to most scholars of later generations, the Chinese people or foreign translators. It would have become lost to the world if Hua-Ching Ni had not rewritten it and put it into simple language. He has practically revived the ancient teaching to make it useful for all people.

This list is made according to date of publication. It offers you another way to study Master Ni's work in a natural order of his spiritual revelation.

1979: *The Complete Works of Lao Tzu*
      The Taoist Inner View of the Universe
      Tao, the Subtle Universal Law
1983: *The Book of Changes and the Unchanging Truth*
      8,000 Years of Wisdom, I
      8,000 Years of Wisdom, II
1984: *Workbook for Spiritual Development*
1985: *The Uncharted Voyage Toward the Subtle Light* (reprinted as
          Awaken to the Great Path and
          Ascend the Spiritual Mountain)
1986: *Footsteps of the Mystical Child*
1987: *The Gentle Path of Spiritual Progress*
      Spiritual Messages from a Buffalo Rider (originally
          part of *Gentle Path of Spiritual Progress*)
1989: *The Way of Integral Life*
      Enlightenment: Mother of Spiritual Independence
      Attaining Unlimited Life
      The Story of Two Kingdoms
1990: *Stepping Stones for Spiritual Success*
      Guide to Inner Light
      Essence of Universal Spirituality
1991: *Internal Growth through Tao*
      Nurture Your Spirits
      Quest of Soul
      Power of Natural Healing
      Eternal Light
      The Key to Good Fortune: Refining Your Spirit
1992: *Attune Your Body with Dao-In*
      Harmony: The Art of Life
      Moonlight in the Dark Night
      Life and Teachings of Two Immortals, Volume I: Kou Hong
      The Mystical Universal Mother
      Ageless Counsel for Modern Times
      Mysticism: Empowering the Spirit Within
      Internal Alchemy: The Natural Way to Immortality
      Golden Message (by Daoshing and Maoshing Ni, based on
          the works of Master Ni, Hua-Ching)
      Esoteric Tao Teh Ching

In addition, the forthcoming books will be compiled from his lecturing and teaching service:

Gentle Path T'ai Chi Ch'uan
Sky Journey T'ai Chi Ch'uan
Infinite Expansion T'ai Chi Ch'uan
Cosmic Tour Ba Gua Zahn
Life and Teachings of Two Immortals, Volume II: Chen Tuan
Immortal Wisdom
The Way, the Truth and the Light
From Diversity to Unity
By the Light of the North Star

BOOKS IN ENGLISH BY MASTER NI

Esoteric Tao Teh Ching - New Publication!
Tao Teh Ching has great profundity in philosophy and spiritual meaning, and can be understood in many ways and on many levels. In this new previously unreleased edition, Master Ni gives instruction for spiritual practices, which includes in-depth information and important techniques for spiritual benefit. 192 pages, Softcover, Stock No. BESOT, $12.95

Golden Message - A Guide to Spiritual Life with Self-Study Program for Learning the Integral Way - *New Publication!*
This volume begins with a traditional treatise by Master Ni's sons about the general nature of spiritual learning and its application for human life and behavior. It is followed by a message from Master Ni and an outline of the Spiritual Self-Study Program and Correspondence Course of the College of Tao. 160 pages, Softcover, Stock No. BGOLD, $11.95

Internal Alchemy: The Natural Way to Immortality - *New Publication!*
Ancient spiritually achieved ones used alchemical terminology metaphorically for human internal energy transformation. Internal alchemy intends for an individual to transform one's emotion and lower energy to be higher energy and to find the unity of life in order to reach the divine immortality. 288 pages, Softcover, Stock No. BALCH, $15.95

Mysticism: Empowering the Spirit Within - *New Publication!*
For more than 8,000 years, mystical knowledge has been passed down by sages. Master Ni introduces spiritual knowledge of the developed ones which does not use the senses or machines like scientific knowledge, yet can know both the entirety of the universe and the spirits. 200 pages, Softcover, Stock No. BMYST2, $13.95

Life and Teaching of Two Immortals, Volume 1: Kou Hong - *New Publication!*
Master Kou Hong was an achieved Master, a healer in Traditional Chinese Medicine and a specialist in the art of refining medicines who was born in 363 A.D. He laid the foundation of later cultural development in China. 176 pages, Softcover, Stock No. BLIF1, $12.95.

Ageless Counsel for Modern Life - *New Publication!*
These sixty-four writings, originally illustrative commentaries on the I Ching, are meaningful and useful spiritual guidance on various topics to enrich your life. Master Ni's delightful poetry and some teachings of esoteric Taoism can be found here as well. 256 pages, Softcover, Stock No. BAGEL, $15.95.

The Mystical Universal Mother
An understanding of both masculine and feminine energies are crucial to understanding oneself, in particular for people moving to higher spiritual evolution. Master Ni focuses upon the feminine through the examples of some ancient and modern women. 240 pages, Softcover, Stock No. BMYST, $14.95

Moonlight in the Dark Night
To attain inner clarity and freedom of the soul, you have to control your emotions. This book contains wisdom on balancing the emotions, including balancing love relationships, so that spiritual achievement becomes possible. 168 pages, Softcover, Stock No. BMOON, $12.95

Harmony - The Art of Life
Harmony occurs when two different things find the point at which they can link together. Master Ni shares valuable spiritual understanding and insight about the ability to bring harmony within one's own self, one's relationships and the world. 208 pages, Softcover, Stock No. BHARM, $14.95

Attune Your Body with Dao-In
The ancients discovered that Dao-In exercises solved problems of stagnant energy, increased their health and lengthened their years. The exercises are also used as practical support for cultivation and higher achievements of spiritual immortality. 144 pages, Softcover with photographs, Stock No. BDAOI, $14.95 Also on VHS, Stock No. VDAOI, $39.95

The Key to Good Fortune: Refining Your Spirit
Straighten Your Way *(Tai Shan Kan Yin Pien)* and The Silent Way of Blessing *(Yin Chia Wen)* are the main guidance for a mature, healthy life. Spiritual improvement can be an integral part of realizing a Heavenly life on earth. 144 pages, Softcover, Stock No. BKEYT, $12.95

Eternal Light
Master Ni presents the life and teachings of his father, Grandmaster Ni, Yo San, who was a spiritually achieved person, healer and teacher, and a source of inspiration to Master Ni. Some deeper teachings and understandings on living a spiritual life and higher achievement are given. 208 pages, Softcover, Stock No. BETER, $14.95

Quest of Soul
Master Ni addresses many concepts about the soul such as saving the soul, improving the soul's quality, the free soul, what happens at death and the universal soul. He guides and inspires the reader into deeper self-knowledge and to move forward to increase personal happiness and spiritual depth. 152 pages, Softcover, Stock No. BQUES, $11.95

Nurture Your Spirits
Master Ni breaks some spiritual prohibitions and presents the spiritual truth he has studied and proven. This truth may help you develop and nurture your own spirits which are the truthful internal foundation of your life being. 176 pages, Softcover, Stock No. BNURT, $12.95

Internal Growth through Tao
Master Ni teaches the more subtle, much deeper sphere of the reality of life that is above the shallow sphere of external achievement. He also clears the confusion caused by some spiritual teachings and guides you in the direction of developing spiritually by growing internally. 208 pages, Softcover, Stock No. BINTE, $13.95

Power of Natural Healing

Master Ni discusses the natural capability of self-healing, information and practices which can assist any treatment method and presents methods of cultivation which promote a healthy life, longevity and spiritual achievement. 230 pages, Softcover, Stock No. BHEAL, $14.95

Essence of Universal Spirituality

In this volume, as an open-minded learner and achieved teacher of universal spirituality, Master Ni examines and discusses all levels and topics of religious and spiritual teaching to help you understand the ultimate truth and enjoy the achievement of all religions without becoming confused by them. 304 pages, Softcover, Stock No. BESSE, $19.95

Guide to Inner Light

Drawing inspiration from the experience of the ancient achieved ones, modern people looking for the true source and meaning of life can find great teachings to direct and benefit them. The invaluable ancient development can teach us to reach the attainable spiritual truth and point the way to the Inner Light. 192 pages, Softcover, Stock No. BGUID, $12.95

Stepping Stones for Spiritual Success

In this volume, Master Ni has taken the best of the traditional teachings and put them into contemporary language to make them more relevant to our time, culture and lives. 160 pages, Softcover, Stock No. BSTEP, $12.95.

The Complete Works of Lao Tzu

The *Tao Teh Ching* is one of the most widely translated and cherished works of literature. Its timeless wisdom provides a bridge to the subtle spiritual truth and aids harmonious and peaceful living. Also included is the *Hua Hu Ching*, a later work of Lao Tzu which was lost to the general public for a thousand years. 212 pages, Softcover, Stock No. BCOMP, $12.95

Order *The Complete Works of Lao Tzu* and the companion *Tao Teh Ching* Cassette Tapes for only $23.00. Stock No. ABTAO.

The Book of Changes and the Unchanging Truth

The legendary classic *I Ching* is recognized as the first written book of wisdom. Leaders and sages throughout history have consulted it as a trusted advisor which reveals the appropriate action in any circumstance. Includes over 200 pages of background material on natural energy cycles, instruction and commentaries. 669 pages, Stock No. BBOOK, Hardcover, $35.00

The Story of Two Kingdoms

This volume is the metaphoric tale of the conflict between the Kingdoms of Light and Darkness. Through this unique story, Master Ni transmits esoteric teachings of Taoism which have been carefully guarded secrets for over 5,000 years. This book is for those who are serious in achieving high spiritual goals. 122 pages, Stock No. BSTOR, Hardcover, $14.50

The Way of Integral Life

This book includes practical and applicable suggestions for daily life, philosophical thought, esoteric insight and guidelines for those aspiring to serve the world. The ancient sages' achievement can assist the growth of your own wisdom and balanced, reasonable life. 320 pages, Softcover, Stock No. BWAYS, $14.00. Hardcover, Stock No. BWAYH, $20.00.

Enlightenment: Mother of Spiritual Independence
The inspiring story and teachings of Master Hui Neng, the father of Zen Buddhism and Sixth Patriarch of the Buddhist tradition, highlight this volume. Hui Neng was a person of ordinary birth, intellectually unsophisticated, who achieved himself to become a spiritual leader. 264 pages, Softcover, Stock No. BENLS, $12.50   Hardcover, Stock No. BENLH, $22.00.

Attaining Unlimited Life
Chuang Tzu was perhaps the greatest philosopher and master of Tao. He touches the organic nature of human life more deeply and directly than do other great teachers. This volume also includes questions by students and answers by Master Ni.   467 pages, Softcover, Stock No. BATTS $18.00; Hardcover, Stock No. BATTH, $25.00.

Special Discount: Order the three classics Way of Integral Life, Enlightenment: Mother of Spiritual Independence *and* Attaining Unlimited Light *in the hardbound editions, Stock No.* BHARD *for $49.95.*

The Gentle Path of Spiritual Progress
This book offers a glimpse into the dialogues between a Master and his students. In a relaxed, open manner, Master Ni, Hua-Ching explains to his students the fundamental practices that are the keys to experiencing enlightenment in everyday life. 290 pages, Softcover, Stock No. BGENT, $12.95.

Spiritual Messages from a Buffalo Rider, A Man of Tao
Our buffalo nature rides on us, whereas an achieved person rides the buffalo. Master Ni gives much helpful knowledge to those who are interested in improving their lives and deepening their cultivation so they too can develop beyond their mundane beings. 242 pages, Softcover, Stock No. BSPIR, $12.95.

8,000 Years of Wisdom, Volume I and II
This two-volume set contains a wealth of practical, down-to-earth advice given by Master Ni over a five-year period. Drawing on his training in Traditional Chinese Medicine, Herbology and Acupuncture, Master Ni gives candid answers to questions on many topics. Volume I includes dietary guidance; 236 pages; Stock No. BWIS1 Volume II includes sex and pregnancy guidance; 241 pages; Stock No. BWIS2. Softcover, each volume $12.50

Special discount: Both Books I and II of 8,000 Years of Wisdom, Stock No. BWIS3, *for $22.00.*

Awaken to the Great Path
Originally the first half of the *Uncharted Voyage Toward the Subtle Light*, this volume offers a clear and direct vision of the spiritual truth of life. It explains many of the subtle truths which are obvious to some but unapparent to others. The Great Path is not the unique teaching, but it can show the way to the integral spiritual truth in every useful level of life. 248 pages, Softcover, Stock No. BAWAK, $14.95

Ascend the Spiritual Mountain
Originally the second half of the *Uncharted Voyage Toward the Subtle Light*, this book offers further spiritual understanding with many invaluable practices which may help you integrate your spiritual self with your daily life. In deep truth, at different times and places, people still have only one teacher: the universal spiritual self itself. 216 pages, Softcover, Stock No. BASCE, $14.95

Footsteps of the Mystical Child
This book poses and answers such questions as: What is a soul? What is wisdom? What is spiritual evolution? to enable readers to open themselves to new realms of understanding and personal growth. Includes true examples about people's internal and external struggles on the path of self-development and spiritual evolution. 166 pages, Softcover, Stock No. BFOOT, $9.50

The Heavenly Way
A translation of the classic Tai Shan Kan Yin Pien (Straighten Your Way) and Yin Chia Wen (The Silent Way of Blessing). The treatises in this booklet are the main guidance for a mature and healthy life. This truth can teach the perpetual Heavenly Way by which one reconnects oneself with the divine nature. 41 pages, Softcover, Stock No. BHEAV, $2.50

Special Discount: Order the Heavenly Way in a set of 10 - great for gifts or giveaways. (One shipping item). BHIV10 $17.50.

Workbook for Spiritual Development
This material summarizes thousands of years of traditional teachings and little-known practices for spiritual development. There are sections on ancient invocations, natural celibacy and postures for energy channeling. Master Ni explains basic attitudes and knowledge that supports spiritual practice. 240 pages, Softcover, Stock No. BWORK, $14.95

Poster of Master Lu
Color poster of Master Lu, Tung Ping (shown on cover of workbook), for use with the workbook or in one's shrine. 16" x 22"; Stock No. PMLTP. $10.95

Order the Workbook for Spiritual Development *and the companion Poster of Master Lu for $18.95.* Stock No. BPWOR.

The Taoist Inner View of the Universe
Master Ni has given all the opportunity to know the vast achievement of the ancient unspoiled mind and its transpiercing vision. This book offers a glimpse of the inner world and immortal realm known to achieved ones and makes it understandable for students aspiring to a more complete life. 218 pages, Softcover, Stock No. BTAOI, $14.95

Tao, the Subtle Universal Law
Most people are unaware that their thoughts and behavior evoke responses from the invisible net of universal energy. To lead a good stable life is to be aware of the universal subtle law in every moment of our lives. This book presents practical methods that have been successfully used for centuries to accomplish this. 165 pages, Softcover, Stock No. TAOS, $7.50

MATERIALS ON NATURAL HEALTH, ARTS AND SCIENCES

BOOKS

101 Vegetarian Delights - *New Publication!* by Lily Chuang and Cathy McNease
A vegetarian diet is a gentle way of life with both physical and spiritual benefits. The Oriental tradition provides helpful methods to assure that a vegetarian diet is well-balanced and nourishing. This book provides a variety of clear and precise recipes ranging from everyday nutrition to exotic and delicious feasts. 176 pages, Softcover, Stock No. B101V, $12.95

The Tao of Nutrition by Maoshing Ni, Ph.D., with Cathy McNease, B.S., M.H. - This book offers both a healing and a disease prevention system through eating habits. This volume contains 3 major sections: theories of Chinese nutrition and philosophy; descriptions of 100 common foods with energetic properties and therapeutic actions; and nutritional remedies for common ailments. 214 pages, Softcover, Stock No. BNUTR, $14.50

Chinese Vegetarian Delights by Lily Chuang
An extraordinary collection of recipes based on principles of traditional Chinese nutrition. For those who require restricted diets or who choose an optimal diet, this cookbook is a rare treasure. Meat, sugar, diary products and fried foods are excluded. 104 pages, Softcover, Stock No. BCHIV, $7.50

Chinese Herbology Made Easy - by Maoshing Ni, Ph.D.
This text provides an overview of Oriental medical theory, in-depth descriptions of each herb category, over 300 black and white photographs, extensive tables of individual herbs for easy reference and an index of pharmaceutical and Pin-Yin names. This book gives a clear, efficient focus to Chinese herbology. 202 pages, Softcover, Stock No. BCHIH, 14.50

Crane Style Chi Gong Book - By Daoshing Ni, Ph.D.
Chi Gong is a set of meditative exercises developed thousands of years ago in China and now practiced for healing purposes. It combines breathing techniques, body movements and mental imagery to guide the smooth flow of energy throughout the body. It may be used with or without the videotape. 55 pages. Stock No. BCRAN. Spiral-bound, $10.95

VIDEO TAPES

Attune Your Body with Dao-In (VHS) - by Master Ni. Dao-In is a series of movements traditionally used for conducting physical energy. The ancients discovered that Dao-In exercise solves problems of stagnant energy, increases health and lengthens one's years, providing support for cultivation and higher achievements of spiritual immortality. Stock No. VDAOI, VHS $39.95

T'ai Chi Ch'uan: An Appreciation (VHS) - by Master Ni.
Master Ni, Hua-Ching presents three styles of T'ai Chi handed down to him through generations of highly developed masters. "Gentle Path," "Sky Journey" and "Infinite

Expansion" are presented uninterrupted in this unique videotape, set to music for observation and appreciation. Stock No. VAPPR. VHS 30 minutes $24.95

Crane Style Chi Gong (VHS) - by Dr. Daoshing Ni, Ph.D.

Chi Gong is a set of meditative exercises practiced for healing chronic diseases, strengthening the body and spiritual enlightenment. Correct and persistent practice will increase one's energy, relieve tension, improve concentration, release emotional stress and restore general well-being. 2 hours, Stock No. VCRAN. $39.95

Eight Treasures (VHS) - By Maoshing Ni, Ph.D.

These exercises help open blocks in your energy flow and strengthen your vitality. It is a complete exercise combining physical stretching, toning and energy-conducting movements coordinated with breathing. Patterned from nature, its 32 movements are an excellent foundation for T'ai Chi Ch'uan or martial arts. 1 hour, 45 minutes. Stock No. VEIGH. $39.95

T'ai Chi Ch'uan I & II (VHS) - By Maoshing Ni, Ph.D.

This exercise integrates the flow of physical movement with that of internal energy in the Taoist style of "Harmony," similar to the long form of Yang-style T'ai Chi Ch'uan. Tai Chi has been practiced for thousands of years to help both physical longevity and spiritual cultivation. 1 hour each. Each video tape $39.95. Order both for $69.95. Stock Nos: Part I, VTAI1; Part II, VTAI2; Set of two, VTAI3.

AUDIO CASSETTES

Invocations for Health, Longevity and Healing a Broken Heart - By Maoshing Ni, Ph.D.

This audio cassette guides the listener through a series of ancient invocations to channel and conduct one's own healing energy and vital force. "Thinking is louder than thunder. The mystical power which creates all miracles is your sincere practice of this principle." 30 minutes, Stock No. AINVO, $9.95

Stress Release with Chi Gong - By Maoshing Ni, Ph.D.

This audio cassette guides you through simple, ancient breathing exercises that enable you to release day-to-day stress and tension that are such a common cause of illness today. 30 minutes. Stock No. ACHIS. $9.95

Pain Management with Chi Gong - By Maoshing Ni, Ph.D.

Using easy visualization and deep-breathing techniques developed over thousands of years, this audio cassette offers methods for overcoming pain by invigorating your energy flow and unblocking obstructions that cause pain. 30 minutes, Stock No. ACHIP. $9.95

Tao Teh Ching Cassette Tapes

This classic work of Lao Tzu has been recorded in this two-cassette set that is a companion to the book translated by Master Ni. Professionally recorded and read by Robert Rudelson. 120 minutes. Stock No. ATAOT. $12.95

Order Master Ni's book, *The Complete Works of Lao Tzu,* and *Tao Teh Ching* Cassette Tapes for only $23.00. Stock No. ABTAO.

How To Order

Name: _____

Address: _____

City: _____ State: _____ Zip: _____

Phone - Daytime: _____ Evening: _____

(We may telephone you if we have questions about your order.)

Qty.	Stock No.	Title/Description	Price Each	Total Price

Total amount for items ordered_____

Sales tax (CA residents only, 8-1/4%)_____

Shipping Charge (see below)_____

Total Amount Enclosed_____

Visa _____ Mastercard _____ Expiration Date _____

Card number:_____

Signature:_____

Shipping: Please give full street address or nearest crossroads. If shipping to more than one address, use separate shipping charges. Please allow 2 - 4 weeks for US delivery and 6 - 10 weeks for foreign surface mail.

By Mail: Complete this form with payment (US funds only, No Foreign Postal Money Orders, please) and mail to: Union of Tao and Man, 1314 Second St. #208, Santa Monica, CA 90401

Phone Orders: (310) 576-1901 - You may leave credit card orders anytime on our answering machine. Please speak clearly and remember to leave your full name and daytime phone number.

Shipping Charges:

Domestic Surface: First item $3.25, each additional, add $.50.
Canada Surface: First item $3.25, each additional, add $1.00.
Canada Air: First item $4.00, each additional, add $2.00
Foreign Surface: First Item $3.50, each additional, add $2.00.
Foreign Air: First item $12.00, each additional, add $7.00.

All foreign orders: Add 5% of your book total to shipping charges to cover insurance.

_____ Please send me your complete catalog.

Thank you for your order

Spiritual Study through the College of Tao

The College of Tao and the Union of Tao and Man were established formally in California in the 1970's. This tradition is a very old spiritual culture of mankind, holding long experience of human spiritual growth. Its central goal is to offer healthy spiritual education to all people of our society. This time-tested tradition values the spiritual development of each individual self and passes down its guidance and experience.

Master Ni carries his tradition from its country of origin to the west. He chooses to avoid making the mistake of old-style religions that have rigid establishments which resulted in fossilizing the delicacy of spiritual reality. He prefers to guide the teachings of his tradition as a school of no boundary rather than a religion with rigidity. Thus, the branches or centers of this Taoist school offer different programs of similar purpose. Each center extends its independent service, but all are unified in adopting Master Ni's work as the foundation of teaching to fulfill the mission of providing spiritual education to all people.

The centers offer their classes, teaching, guidance and practices on building the groundwork for cultivating a spiritually centered and well-balanced life. As a person obtains the correct knowledge with which to properly guide himself or herself, he or she can then become more skillful in handling the experiences of daily life. The assimilation of good guidance in one's practical life brings about different stages of spiritual development.

Any interested individual is welcome to join and learn to grow for yourself. Or you just might like to take a few classes in which you are interested. You might like to visit the center or take classes near where you live, or you may be interested in organizing a center or study group based on the model of existing centers. In that way, we all work together for the spiritual benefit of all people. We do not require any religious type of commitment.

The College of Tao also offers a Self-Study program based on Master Ni's books and videotapes. The course outline and details of how to participate are given in his book, *The Golden Message*. The Self-Study program gives people an opportunity to study the learning of Tao at their own speed, for those who wish to study on their own or are too far from a center.

The learning is life. The development is yours. The connection of study may be helpful, useful and serviceable, directly to you.

- -

Mail to: Union of Tao and Man, 1314 Second Street #208, Santa Monica, CA 90401

____ I wish to be put on the mailing list of the Union of Tao and Man to be notified of classes, educational activities and new publications.

Name:_____

Address:_____

City:_____ State:_____ Zip:_____

Herbs Used by Ancient Taoist Masters

The pursuit of everlasting youth or immortality throughout human history is an innate human desire. Long ago, Chinese esoteric Taoists went to the high mountains to contemplate nature, strengthen their bodies, empower their minds and develop their spirit. From their studies and cultivation, they gave China alchemy and chemistry, herbology and acupuncture, the I Ching, astrology, martial arts and T'ai Chi Ch'uan, Chi Gong and many other useful kinds of knowledge.

Most important, they handed down in secrecy methods for attaining longevity and spiritual immortality. There were different levels of approach; one was to use a collection of food herb formulas that were only available to highly achieved Taoist masters. They used these food herbs to increase energy and heighten vitality. This treasured collection of herbal formulas remained within the Ni family for centuries.

Now, through Traditions of Tao, the Ni family makes these foods available for you to use to assist the foundation of your own positive development. It is only with a strong foundation that expected results are produced from diligent cultivation.

As a further benefit, in concert with the Taoist principle of self-sufficiency, Traditions of Tao offers the food herbs along with the Union of Tao and Man's publications in a distribution opportunity for anyone serious about financial independence.

Send to: *Traditions of Tao*
                1314 Second Street #208
                Santa Monica, CA 90401

Please send me a Traditions of Tao brochure.

Name _____

Address_____

City_____State_____Zip_____

Phone (day)_____(night)_____

Yo San University of Traditional Chinese Medicine

"Not just a medical career, but a life-time commitment to raising one's spiritual standard."

Thank you for your support and interest in our publications and services. It is by your patronage that we continue to offer you the practical knowledge and wisdom from this venerable Taoist tradition.

Because of your sustained interest in Taoism, in January 1989 we formed Yo San University of Traditional Chinese Medicine, a non-profit educational institution under the direction of founder Master Ni, Hua-Ching. Yo San University is the continuation of 38 generations of Ni family practitioners who handed down knowledge and wisdom from father to son. Its purpose is to train and graduate practitioners of the highest caliber in Traditional Chinese Medicine, which includes acupuncture, herbology and spiritual development.

We view Traditional Chinese Medicine as the application of spiritual development. Its foundation is the spiritual capability to know life, to diagnose a person's problem and how to cure it. We teach students how to care for themselves and other, emphasizing the integration of traditional knowledge and modern science. Yo San University offers a complete Master's degree program approved by the California State Department of Education that provides an excellent education in Traditional Chinese Medicine and meets all requirements for state licensure.

We invite you to inquire into our university for a creative and rewarding career as a holistic physician. Classes are also open to persons interested only in self-enrichment. For more information, please fill out the form below and send it to:

Yo San University
of Traditional Chinese Medicine
1314 Second Street
Santa Monica, CA 90401

☐ Please send me information on the Masters degree program in Traditional Chinese Medicine.

☐ Please send me information on health workshops and seminars.

☐ Please send me information on continuing education for acupuncturists and health professionals.

Name _____

Address_____

City_____State_____Zip_____

Phone(day)_____(evening)_____

Index